HOW TO CRUSH
SELF-DOUBT
AND GAIN REAL CONFIDENCE

By Corrina Thurston

Onion River Press
Burlington, Vermont

Disclaimer: *This book is not intended to provide and does not constitute medical, legal, or other professional advice. The content in this book is designed to support, not replace, medical or psychiatric treatment. Please seek professional care if you believe you have a condition.*

Onion River Press
191 Bank Street
Burlington, VT 05401

ISBN: 978-1-949066-62-3

Library of Congress Control Number: 2021900630

www.corrinathurston.com

To Daniel, my partner in this crazy life. I appreciate the many, many things you do for me. You are wonderful.

To Josiah, my sweet boy. I love you so much.

To my family, my support system. I couldn't do it without you.

What Others Are Saying About *How To Crush Self-Doubt and Gain Real Confidence*:

"This book was easy to read and honestly, the best self help book I have seen so far, and I've tried to read a lot of them. This is the first one where I read all the way to the end and found myself taking notes. So many helpful ideas. I especially enjoyed the section on the Imposter Syndrome."

- Dr. Nancy Fuller

*"**How To Crush Self-Doubt and Gain Real Confidence** is a wonderful, straightforward book on improving your confidence. Corrina relates to her readers by giving examples of her own struggles throughout this book, which helps to explain how many of her confidence-boosting techniques work. This book covers a wide variety of issues, from social anxiety, work anxiety, creative anxiety, and depression."*

- Misty Allen – Artist, Drafter, Etcher

*"Corrina Thurston has done it again with her new book, **How To Crush Self-Doubt and Gain Real Confidence**. Corrina packs a punch and gives the reader exactly what they need along with examples. Would you like to know tips on building your self-esteem? Then read this book. Would you like to know how to have more confidence in yourself? Then read this book. Would you like to be seen as more professional? Then read this book. The useful and ready-to-use information is jam-packed into this book. Happy reading."*

- Lisa Perfetti

"Easy to read format and succinct, Corrina's life experiences and her continuing recovery provide a wealth of information to its reader. Corrina's unabashed style of writing is like having her right there in the room with you, as she personally coaches the reader in the strategies that have worked for her in the past and in moving forward on a daily basis."

- Anita Michele – Artist

*"I plan to read Corrina's book, **How To Crush Self-Doubt and Gain Real Confidence**, over and over again! I wish this book had been around when I was younger. But – I'm grateful to have it now, knowing it's never too late. There are so many wonderful nuggets I want to absorb, especially to help me overcome chronic low self-esteem and Imposter Syndrome. I'm glad Corrina is in this world, and I am so grateful to her for writing such a wonderful guide!"*

- Lorri Dixon

*"**How To Crush Self-doubt And Gain Real Confidence** is an easy-to-read book that will help the reader in many areas of their life. As well as the many useful nuggets of information there are many chapters to assist the reader through the maze of problems associated with self-doubt and the lack of confidence. Corrina covers these with her usual ease that so benefits the reader. Logically laid out this helps the reader to either read the book sequentially or in bits as and when. I certainly wish this book was around years ago when I was younger as this would certainly have improved my life at that time. I would definitely recommend this book to all who suffer from self-doubt or who lack confidence."*

- RobboPetes' Artwork

"This book is essential for artists as we need to remember our worth. Corrina has captured our everyday thoughts and addressed them in a way that shows she understands, being a creative soul herself. She speaks directly to our fears and talks us through them as she shares her experiences with the same topics that make us doubt ourselves. A must read and reread as we need the little reminders that we are enough."

- Janet Soavi

"I went into Corrina's 3rd book hesitantly. Thinking, hmmm what a change from her other two books and self-help at that. BUT, she has done an excellent job in given straight advice to the reader. The best part of the book, Corrina sharing her own struggles and journey to where she is now. It solidifies for the reader that she understands and brings hope."

- Dawn Whitmore, The "Old Barn" Lady

"Corrina provides her readers with real, useable techniques that can be used to help improve difficult aspects of life. Her writing style is down to earth and clearly understood; allowing the reader to take full advantage of her teaching."

- Christian Schoenig

*"This book, **How To Crush Self-Doubt and Gain Real Confidence**, is full of nuggets of wisdom. Corrina Thurston is authentic and vulnerable. She writes in a very engaging manner about the battles for self acceptance, practical ways to calm and encourage oneself, and ways to break the cycle of getting overwhelmed and paralyzed by the negative false messages of American culture.*"

- Grace Buchanan

Table Of Contents:

1
I Don't Know

I'm curious, when did we decide it wasn't okay to say, "I don't know?"

There's not a single person in this world that knows everything. Not knowing something is what drives our curiosity and urge to learn. So why do we feel uncomfortable and ashamed to say those three words?

My significant other has a larger vocabulary than I do. He's also better at spelling and grammar, he knows another language and I don't, he's much better at geography, current events, sports knowledge, socializing, and any number of things. When we first started dating I found myself intimidated by some of this. What if he found out I don't know as much as he knows? Would I be less attractive if he knew I was just nodding along sometimes?

When our relationship started we both knew we were searching for something serious, a relationship that would last. Knowing that, we didn't want to waste any time and I decided to be completely honest and forthright and not try to cover up my flaws. I told him within our first few dates that I needed a lot of attention, I am sarcastic and moody, and that I need to have cats in my life. He told me he wanted to have kids someday and not wanting kids would probably be a deal-breaker.

Duly noted.

So the next time he said a word I didn't know, I stopped him and said I didn't know what that meant. He quickly explained it to me and then continued on and that was that.

We both have our strengths, and our weaknesses. We both know things the other doesn't. It doesn't matter. When one of us is talking about something the other is unfamiliar with, we just explain it and keep going. We don't think less of one another, we just use it as an opportunity to teach and learn.

The same should be true of any situation.

If you're in a room full of people and they're talking about something you don't quite understand, but everyone else seems to be nodding along, raise your hand and say you're not familiar with what they're talking about and ask them to explain it. If you've never heard of something, then how can you be familiar with it? There's nothing wrong with that, even if you are the only one feeling left behind in the conversation (which you might not be, you might just be the only one to admit it openly).

Don't let yourself get left behind. If you're not sure about something, ASK. That way you can stay with the conversation or meeting and feel less uncomfortable.

Do this with confidence. Don't be apologetic; you have nothing for which to be sorry. There's nothing wrong with asking questions or wanting to stay on the same page as everyone else, so simply state what you don't understand and ask them to explain.

Raises hand to get attention

"Excuse me, but I don't quite understand what you mean when you say the acronym GRSEO. Can you explain that quickly so I can get up to speed? Thanks."

Say it politely, but with expectation. It's not a question, you're telling them what to do. There's no hesitation in your voice, no doubt. This is what you need done, so if they could please do it, that would be great.

If anyone mocks you or says anything derogative or gives you an incredulous look, either ignore them or quickly explain how it's impossible to know something you've never heard or learned about before.

When you admit to not knowing something, it can develop into a deeper form of respect from those around you. You want to learn. Plus, you not knowing whatever it is doesn't mean you're any less confident. If you were put in a different situation, you might know lots of things they don't know.

The more confidently you can say anything (while still being polite and considerate, not arrogant) the more people are going to trust you and like you and respect you.

Then there are times when someone will ask you a question, like during an interview, and you won't know the answer. That's okay too. I say, "I don't know" all the time. Sometimes I follow it up by explaining I'd need to calculate numbers to be sure of something. Other times I say I have no experience with whatever they're asking about, so I have no form of reference. Or sometimes they're asking a question they think has an answer, but it's actually that THEY don't quite understand what I do.

No matter the situation, if I'm asked a direct question for which I don't have an answer, I tell them I don't know and then try to briefly explain why. Or, maybe I can't answer this question, but I can answer this similar one, which might be helpful...

Whatever you do, DO NOT MAKE STUFF UP.

Don't try to impress anyone. Trying to impress someone is not confidence. Confidence is driven by realizing that if you impress someone, great, you've just found one of your people in this world, and if not, oh well.

Confidence is basing your words and actions on yourself, not those around you. When you are confident, you act the same way no matter who is nearby, you don't try to change something about yourself to impress certain people.

Remember when you make things up or guess it has the potential to backfire. There's nothing wrong with not knowing. Sometimes it's a matter of not knowing at that moment but being able to look something up and get back to them. That's fine.

It may sound strange to say "don't make stuff up." You might be thinking, well of course not, why would I? Here's why

I mention this: even those of us who are wonderful people can be influenced by our fear of judgment and act like we know something when we really don't. It happens all the time. If you're nervous and someone asks you a question, you might respond even though you're actually not sure. It's a gut reaction to cover up a "flaw" of not knowing.

It's instinct and it's one that we've all likely been guilty of at one point or another, but you need to catch it. It's not good for you or the other person. Most of the time it sets higher expectations on you, and you might not be able to meet them.

I'm now considered an "expert" in a number of fields, and I say I don't know all the time. I don't need to be apologetic about it (which is hard for someone who suffers with unnecessary guilt); it's just stating a fact.

I don't know.

I'm not sure, let me get back to you.

I'm not positive, can you explain it?

I'm not sure what you mean.

I don't quite understand how this works.

Once you start to recognize there's no need to get flustered or uncomfortable or feel ashamed, it takes on a whole new light. Not knowing doesn't mean you're less than anyone else, it means this is an opportunity to learn something. That's it.

It's an opportunity to *learn*.

Jump on it.

2

Knowledge Builds Confidence

I've given two speeches recently. One was in front of about 35 people, was three minutes long, and was not filmed or really being critiqued in any way. The other was a TEDx Talk on a large stage in front of 450 people, with multiple cameras filming it so they can put it online afterwards for potentially millions of people to see.

Now, logically, the second of the two speeches should have made me more nervous. It was longer and the stakes were much higher, not to mention the audience was significantly larger.

But that wasn't the case.

The first speech was the one that had me quivering like a leaf.

Why?

Because I went into that first speech with a lot less knowledge than I did the second speech.

For the first speech, I would be talking at a location I had never been to before. I wasn't sure if I'd be on a stage or not, have a microphone or not, or how it would be set up. I had no idea who else would be speaking, how many people would be in the audience, or what it would be like.

In the next chapter I talk a little about visualization and how helpful that can be, but for this first speech, I couldn't do that. I didn't know what to visualize! This made me more nervous because I didn't have any idea what to expect.

For the second speech, I rehearsed on location multiple times. I knew what to expect and I knew exactly how to visualize how the night would play out. I knew the other speakers, I knew the venue, I knew how the sound system and lighting would be set up, etc. This made it easy for me to visualize giving my speech while I was practicing at home 8,578,539,455 times.

I also had more time to prepare for the second speech than I did the first.

The more you practice something, the more comfortable you'll feel with it. Instead of having only a few days to write and memorize my speech, like I did with the first one, I had months of preparation time.

What this goes to show you is that KNOWLEDGE can be a huge factor in your confidence level.

Think about something you do or somewhere you go where you have confidence. It might be making a certain meal, a sport, or driving in an area where you are very familiar. Why do you feel confident doing those things? It's because **confidence is built on prior knowledge and experience**.

When you're driving in an area with which you're familiar, there's very little stress. But when you start driving in a city or area with which you are unfamiliar and you can't find a parking spot and you're driving around and getting confused by one-way streets and how to get where you want to go…then it can become extremely stressful.

If you're like me, your heart rate might have jumped a little just reading about the above situation.

Sometimes when you know you're going to be driving somewhere unfamiliar, or doing something you've never done before, the stress can start to build in anticipation, well before the actual event takes place. You're anxiety climbs and you start to dwell on it, which makes you even more nervous and your confidence can plummet.

The more you know about a situation, the more confidence you'll have. This means looking at a map BEFORE you leave the house. Or watching a video of someone doing the activity you're about to try before you do it.

It could also mean reading up on certain subjects before an interaction. For example, job interviews can be stressful. You might be feeling under-qualified or nervous that you'll answer a question wrong, etc. Therefore, before you get to the interview I suggest you do some research. Research the company, research the person interviewing you, research the person who had the job before you if that's applicable, etc.

The more you research, the more confident you can be when interacting with your interviewer. If you show them you've researched their company by describing how you connect with their mission statement or you were really impressed with some project they did in the past, that can go a long way.

The more you know, the more you can comfortably talk about something. The more you can comfortably talk about something, the more confident you'll be in the conversation.

Research can also mean if you're going to speak at an event, you look up what the event was like last year so you know what to expect. It could mean searching through Google to learn about something before it happens. It could even mean traveling to a location as a "dry run" so you know where you're going and feel more confident about getting there.

Research can also come in the form of talking to other people. Ask a mentor, friend, or colleague what they think about a situation or event or whatever it is that's making you nervous. Ask for advice. Ask for recommendations. Ask for input.

There's nothing wrong with being nervous. In fact, there are many times in your life where you'll want to be at least a little nervous, as it keeps you alert and prepared. Thinking about it like this can help: "I'm not nervous, I'm excited!" Your body has some of the same chemical and bodily reactions to excitement and fear, so maybe you can trick yourself into believing it's really excitement!

The worst thing you can do is let your nerves overtake your self-confidence in a way that makes you struggle to maintain composure, want to cancel your plans, or doesn't allow you to enjoy yourself because you're too busy worrying.

Trust me, I've done all those things. My anxiety used to be so bad that I would have panic attacks in my own home, by myself. Going out to run errands was next to impossible, and there are times I actually put food back on the shelf in a grocery store and walked out without anything because I couldn't get myself to walk through the check out lane.

That's how bad it was.

I spent more of my life at that time IN panic mode than OUT of it. I never felt relaxed at all.

Now, however, I've been interviewed on TV, I give speeches and workshops, I host events, I have been interviewed on podcasts, radio, and for print media, etc.

So when I say the techniques I lay out in this book can work, I've actually lived it. I know what that incapacitating fear, guilt, depression, and anxiety feels like, and I want to try and help you. I don't want you to feel that way.

It'll take time. It'll take training with these techniques.

And it'll take PRACTICE.

3
Practice

There was a joke I saw online the other day that talked about finding a book in the library that said, **How To Be Good At Anything**, and it only had one page inside with one word written on it: Practice.

I love that, mostly because it's true.

Now, not all practice is created equal. You and I can practice something the same amount of time and not be at an equivalent level of competence. For example, I learned how to draw very quickly, much more quickly than is usual, and yet my learning curve for cooking is…a bit more of a challenge.

Believe me when I say, nobody is confident and great at something without at least a bit of practice, and the more you practice something, the more confidence you'll gain.

I gave my TEDx Talk very recently, so it's on my mind as I'm writing this. It was a huge event and of course it was nerve-wracking. When I found out I would be one of the speakers for this event, months before it happened, I came very close to having my first panic attack in years and had to stop what I was doing to go for a walk and use just about all the coping mechanisms I've found to help calm myself down.

I was petrified but I knew it was a great opportunity, so how could I turn it down?

I couldn't. Not if I wanted to grow and challenge myself.

So after practicing my calming techniques (which are explained in later chapters of this book), I got busy figuring out what I would talk about and preparing myself for the event.

I can't tell you how much I practiced my speech. I knew on the night of the event my anxiety was going to be high, which meant my memory was going to be struggling to work over the panic in my brain.

So I practiced, and I practiced, and I practiced.

While I was driving I would be giving my speech, over and over again in the car. I would stand in the middle of my living room again and again and practice my speech to my cats and couches, pretending they were the crowd. I would rehearse it in the shower, in my head while I was lying in bed, while I was cooking, walking, drawing, and cleaning. There was hardly a time in the few weeks leading up to the event that I wasn't practicing my speech.

What did this do for me?

All that practice made it so when I got up on that stage and was being blinded by that light and standing in front of all those people and cameras, I had my speech memorized so well it was practically on auto-flow.

Of course I was nervous and I dreaded making a mistake and forgetting a line, but my anxiety was dampened because I had done such a diligent job practicing and rehearsing and visualizing how that night would go.

You can't expect yourself to give a killer speech or do anything well without practice.

But let's get something straight. Practice makes…better, not perfect.

I like the sentiment behind the phrase, "practice makes perfect," but I hate the word perfect. You shouldn't strive for perfection because if that's your expectation, you're bound to be disappointed. Not to mention what others think is perfect, you might still see as having flaws. If you're an artist you know exactly what I mean. As the creator, you can see all the different mistakes in your own work, but your audience doesn't necessarily see them, and to them, it could be perfect.

So don't strive for perfect. Strive for better than you were before. Strive for always improving.

Perfect is an unreasonable expectation to have and can fuel some of your anxiety. Something doesn't have to be perfect to be effective. Something doesn't have to be perfect to have an impact, to be great, or to help other people.

So next time you're feeling a lack of confidence, remember to practice. Sometimes that means rehearsing, sometimes that means trying something again and again. Sometimes it means visualizing a situation and what you might do if something goes wrong and how you might avoid that or gloss over a mistake if it happens.

The more prepared you are, the more confident you'll be.

This is true for anything.

Worried about making a new dish for a party and not having it come out well? Do a couple practice runs in the weeks leading up to it. Not feeling confident about an upcoming interview? Do your research so you have as much information as you can get and then visualize what it might be like and practice answering questions you think they might ask.

Visualizing a situation is one of the best things you can do if you can't actually practice something. For some situations you can practice the actual thing again and again until you get better. For example, you can go shoot a basketball over and over again to practice so you're better when you're playing a game with your friends. However, when it's an interview or an event you're hosting, there isn't a specific thing you can physically practice on your own to help. Instead you have to visualize what it might be like and how you can succeed.

You might also want to visualize what it might be like if you DON'T do a good job. This way, if you make a mistake during the actual situation, you've prepared for it by visualizing what that might be like and thinking ahead of time about ways to move past it or minimize a mistake.

What if I fall on stage? I'll just stand up, laugh it off, and keep going.

What if I stutter answering the interviewers question? I'll apologize quickly, saying that I'm a little nervous, breathe, and then try again.

What if I air-ball a shot during a basketball game? I'll just shrug and try everything I can to get the ball back on defense to make up for it.

What if I make a really obvious spelling mistake in my cover letter? I'll either send them a new copy or just leave it since it's already been sent and hope it doesn't deter them.

4
Failure

Let's talk about one of the things that makes our self-confidence the lowest and our fears the most overwhelming: Failure.

We all fear failure, and the judgment that comes with it. Judgment from ourselves, from our loved ones, and from people we've never even met before. To fail is to be wrong, to do something wrong, to mess up, make a mistake, and make a fool of ourselves.

But guess what? WE ALL FAIL.

We don't just fail once, either, we fail all the time. At least I do. Big failures, small failures, and everything in between. I've never met someone who hasn't failed.

So why do we allow the fear of failure to hold so much power over us? If it's so common, then why is it such a gripping force holding us back? Why do we allow it to matter so much?

No one starts out being perfect at anything. It takes work and it takes failures to learn how to do something well, and even then there is still the risk of failure and mistakes.

If you're not good at something right away, it doesn't make you bad at it, it just means you haven't had enough practice. Everything takes practice, and with more practice comes more knowledge, experience, and confidence.

The definition of failure is different for everyone. Therefore, something you see as a failure, another person might not!

Let's say you're going to give a speech. You have it

memorized but then when you're in front of your crowd you lose your place and have to fill with something different until you find your way back to the original speech. You might think that was a failure but your audience didn't know what the original speech said. They might not know you lost your place and were improvising. To them, it might have seemed like a success!

If you still got the point across in your speech and were fluid most of the time, or if you were still heartfelt the whole time, they might still love your speech. You knew you went off your script, but they might not have even noticed.

Maybe you try painting for the first time and you end up hating the painting you create, thinking it's not realistic enough, or the colors didn't come out the way you wanted. Well, again, your audience might not know what you were trying to do, they only know what's in front of them as the finished product and it might appeal to them just the way it is. Even though it's not quite what you were hoping it would be, they could think it's amazing.

Still worried people are going to judge you too harshly with something you have coming up? Why not let them know you're a newbie? If you let people know you're new to this, it'll lower their expectations and make you a little more comfortable. However, and this is a big HOWEVER, please only say it ONCE. If you're going on and on about how you're new to this, it'll backfire and you'll lose their attention, patience, and interest. If you say quickly, however, that this is one of your first times, so to bear with you, and then do whatever it is you're doing, it might help.

Example: "This is the first workshop I've taught, so I'm excited to have you all be a part of it...."

The risk of failure is higher when you're doing something new. That's part of what makes it so interesting and exciting, and also what makes it so frightening.

First of all, kudos to you for trying new things! Here you are, stepping outside your comfort zone to try this new thing, despite the risk, and even though it can feel terrifying, doing things like that on a regular basis can help boost your overall self-confidence. (See

22

chapter on The Comfort Zone.)

I feel bad for the people who don't fail on a regular basis. It makes me wonder what they're doing with their lives. What have they learned? The most memorable lessons I've had are from failures and mistakes I've made. Failing made me learn certain things more quickly. It keeps me humble, makes me spend more time planning things out for success, and allows me to connect better with other people.

If you're not failing at least once in a while, I'd venture to guess you're not going outside your comfort zone enough.

Every risk you take has the potential to fail. What we forget sometimes – due to the cloud coverage that is our fear of failure – is that it also has the potential to be a success.

There are even times when a failure is a blessing in disguise. For example, not getting one job might mean you are then available for another job that opens up later, which is more suitable for you but would have been off limits if you'd been accepted to the first job.

There are even times when you will do everything right, but whatever it is still won't succeed. Not all failures are your fault. It doesn't always mean you did something wrong.

The trick with failure is to move on as quickly as possible. Don't let yourself dwell on something that went wrong, instead look at the situation analytically. What went wrong? How did it go wrong? What could have been done better? What can you LEARN from the situation to use for future situations? Is there any benefit from this failure?

Think critically, without beating yourself up, and then move on to the next thing. This is exactly the advice I give in my first book, **How To Build Your Art Business with Limited Time or Energy**, when I talk about rejection. Take what you can from it, learn from it, apply that knowledge to future projects/proposals, and then move on as quickly as you can.

You don't have time to wallow.

Failure and rejection are a part of life and we need to find ways to make ourselves react with less emotion toward those two

23

things and more analytical thought.

Laugh it off when you misspeak in a presentation. Let people know you're new at painting before you show them your work if it makes you more comfortable. Ask the HR person why you didn't get the job and if they have any recommendations or advice for you to learn from. Turn your failed baking effort into a viral "Nailed it!" image online.

No matter what your "failure," allow yourself to cry and yell and be angry or whatever you need for 15 minutes, and then pull yourself together, wash your face, and figure out what's next.

There's no failure you can't get past.

There's nothing wrong with making mistakes.

Every failure can turn into another opportunity and/or lesson.

5
Learning To Say No

I was completely finished writing this book, had edited it once over, and then realized I was missing something important: learning how to say NO.

It sounds so simple. It's only a two-letter word. People say it all the time!

Yet it can be challenging for those of us with self-doubt to say this word as often as we should.

Why?

Because saying no can hurt someone's feelings. You know, you've been there at one point or another. Saying no could also let someone down. It could cause a riff in a relationship. It could become an argument. It could be seen as an insult.

And so on.

It's hard to say no because you're so busy trying to please everyone and putting them ahead of yourself that you forget how important it is for you to manage your own time and energy. You forget how important it is to respect your own limitations.

It's not just important for you, either, it's important for those around you. When you give and you give and you give, you are not leaving enough energy for yourself. You need some of that energy to help maintain your own mental and physical health, which will make you function better for both yourself and your loved ones, as well as your work and the rest of your life.

Putting yourself first isn't selfish, in fact it's the opposite. Putting yourself and your own well-being first means you know you will be a better person for those around you – your family, your friends, your coworkers, your clients – when you're well-rested, happier, healthier, and less overwhelmed.

Saying no is an important and often overlooked part of developing your confidence.

It's okay to feel badly when you say it. It's okay to wish you could say yes.

There are times, however, no matter how badly we want to say yes to something, we need to say no.

No, I don't have the energy to go out.

No, I can't meet that deadline.

No, I can't do that project for you for free.

No, I'm not up to making dinner tonight, can you please do it?

It's not that you CAN'T do that project for that person for free – something artists like me get asked all the time – it's that if you did, you'd be taking valuable time and energy away from the things you need to do that DO make you money, and you have to eat! You have to pay rent! You have car payments and school loans and all sorts of bills. Therefore, it is completely reasonable to prioritize the projects that make you money over those that don't.

If you can confidently (and empathetically) say no and explain why, not only will you be doing a better job at respecting your limitations, those around you will start doing a better job too. Your boss might not keep giving you unreasonable deadlines. Your spouse might start to understand that sometimes you need a break from certain chores or the kids or whatever it is. People might stop asking you to do stuff for free and offer to pay you for your services and time.

When you're overwhelmed with tasks, it means you're not functioning at your optimal levels. Being overwhelmed means there's too much going on and you need to slow it down. It means you need to say no to something.

If you've reached the point of being overwhelmed, you might even need to say no to something for which you've already said yes, which is even harder.

This also means you need to learn how to prioritize, which is easier said than done. Sometimes it's hard to tell what project you should work on because you have no idea how they're going to be received by the world. Or perhaps you had to push aside some family time because of a big deadline at work, but did it feel right to you at the time? Was that deadline really more important than your family time in the long run?

I just saw an interesting article with Nora Roberts where someone asked her how she balances her work life and her home life. Her response is what I found insightful: She said you're constantly juggling balls. Some are plastic, some are glass. If you drop a plastic one, it'll bounce and be okay. If you drop a glass one, it'll shatter. Therefore, when you're prioritizing what you need to do for work or family, try to see which ball out of the 57 we're constantly juggling – this deadline, school play, dinner with family, that work project, helping kids with homework, chores – is glass and needs to be taken care of and which one is plastic and can be dropped for a bit. Sometimes in order to catch a glass ball, you have to drop a plastic one.

Imagine you're lying on your deathbed and thinking about your life. What would be your biggest regrets? Usually it's working too much, not spending enough time with family and friends, and not having enough fun/being happy.

These things can be changed now, before you get to that point. You can pull back and take a sky-view of your life and how you use your time and energy and decide right now if it's working for you, or if you need to start saying no more often.

Sometimes we say no to a good thing so that we can say yes to something even better.

No matter what you're saying no to, it can be a challenge. There's a lot of emotional reaction on both sides – the recipient and the person saying it – for the word no.

The more confident you are, the easier saying no will become. It's not because your confidence will make you someone who doesn't care about the consequences of saying no, it's because you start prioritizing your own energy and respect your limitations instead of constantly pushing too hard and getting run over with everything you have to do.

Have confidence that you're making the right decision and putting your health and well-being first.

Building up your confidence will help you realize how important you are. It's better for you, plus those around you, if you plan things out and don't get overworked. You'll do a much better job on the things you ARE doing, if you don't let yourself get overwhelmed. Instead of being at 40% of your ability doing 10 projects, you'll be at 100% of your ability doing 5 projects, and those projects will be much better and you'll feel much better.

Sometimes this means saying no to things you desperately want to do. You have to say no to yourself, and I think sometimes that's the hardest. I had to do this yesterday. I've had a migraine all week and all I wanted to do was go grab some groceries. I got dressed and ready to go, but I could feel my head was borderline and I knew deep down that if I grabbed my son and went out, it would make my head worse and I'd end up in the middle of the grocery store with a debilitating migraine and my 9-month-old son.

It's even worse when some cool new opportunity comes up, but you know you don't have the energy to do it. You might have to say no and move on, wondering if it was the right choice, wondering what that opportunity could have turned into. This can be incredibly upsetting. I have to do this all the time due to my time and health restraints, but you can have confidence that you made the right decision.

You need to have the confidence to put yourself first. You deserve it, but like I've said, it makes life better for those around you too. Saying no now might mean you can say yes to something else later. Saying no means you have more energy, enthusiasm, and ability to put toward the things for which you've been able to say yes.

It's the old saying "You can't pour from an empty cup."

Don't drain yourself by trying to accomplish too much at once, leaving nothing left of yourself.

This is especially common for parents. Sometimes you need a break and time for yourself and that's 100% okay. You'll be better for your kids in the long run if you feel better when you ARE with them rather than just trying to push through each day.

If someone makes you feel bad for saying no, you know what to do, right? You stand up for yourself. You explain why you're saying no so they can try to see your viewpoint and explain that saying no now means you'll be better later.

Communicate.

Be open and honest.

Everyone has limitations.

You can't say yes to everything.

You need to learn to prioritize and figure out which balls you're juggling are plastic and can be dropped once in a while, and which ones are glass and should be prioritized so they don't shatter.

You don't need to go through life overworked and overwhelmed, always on the edge of some sort of breakdown, just pushing through it all.

Prioritize YOU. The rest will fall into place once you do.

6
Recognize Your Value

A lot of self-doubt comes from comparison. We're a social species, so it makes sense that we're constantly looking at each other and analyzing how other people do things, and impressed when someone else does something great. That's fine, and we should all be happy for one another in our successes.

However...just because someone else is killing it and getting lots of great opportunities and doing lots of amazing things doesn't mean you aren't also great.

Your view of yourself shouldn't change or have anything to do with other people. You should aim to be the same person with the same values and the same personality no matter who you are around. That's what confidence really is. It's recognizing that you don't have to change or cover up or try to be something you're not, no matter who you are around.

There's no need to compare yourself to others, it's only comparing your present self with your past self that matters.

Are you improving? Are you stronger, better, and more well-rounded than you used to be? Are you trying to learn from your mistakes? Are you trying to do your best?

That's all that matters.

Comparison is a rabbit-hole you don't want to fall down.

We're typically our own harshest critic. This means when you compare yourself to the people around you, what you're noticing is all the good things about them and all the inadequacies about yourself. That's not a fair assessment. Not to mention, what you can't see is the person you're looking at might be feeling the exact same way about you and you have no idea.

No matter what, YOU HAVE VALUE.

You have a unique perspective that has been developed (and continues to shift and change with new experiences) over your lifetime from a unique set of circumstances. Just by looking at you, no one knows the many things you've been through, your successes, your failures, or the difficult times you've gotten through.

You can't see that about them either.

So let's stop judging each other about one thing or another because we're forgetting there is a WHOLE person in there who has experienced things we might not be able to see or imagine.

For example, you'd never know by looking at me that I spent over six years mostly bedridden with a chronic, 24/7, excruciating migraine, fatigue, pain, anxiety, hallucinations, etc. You'd never know I have been suicidal. You'd never know how suffocating my self-doubt used to be. You'd never know how much mental training has gone into making me the person I am today.

Let's stop judging ourselves so harshly too, because no matter what anyone says, you have successfully made it through 100% of the days you've been alive, good, bad, or ugly, and your experiences and your unique perspective are worthy.

So if you're doubting your ability or you're in a room with people who are in some way more qualified, or smarter, or more experienced than you, you should CONGRATULATE yourself.

First of all, you've made it in the room too. Something got you there, in that room full of exceptional people, so kudos to you for being one of them!

Secondly, it says a lot about you that you've put yourself in a room where you don't feel like one of the smartest people. That takes courage.

It's also an excellent growth opportunity for you.

You don't learn and grow when you're the smartest person

31

in the room, for that you need people around you who will challenge you and have different perspectives and say and do things that will help you learn. To learn and grow, you don't WANT to be the smartest or most talented person in the room.

Cut yourself some slack and use this experience as a growth and learning opportunity. And remember that just because you have a different perspective, it doesn't mean yours is any less interesting or valid.

I'm an artist. My artwork started out as a hobby, a therapeutic activity when I was extremely sick for all those years and stuck in bed. Eventually, after I started treatment and began to see a little bit of progress in my health, I decided to turn it into a business.

The doubters were everywhere.

My own friends kept asking me what I was going to do for a "real job" when I was finally healthy again.

People at my art exhibits would sometimes belittle my illness, saying it wasn't real, or that I should be healthy by now, or that I didn't "look sick."

People asked me to do things for free because it was "just a drawing," not realizing that each drawing I do takes about 100 hours or more, and I have to work in small time chunks due to my health so they can take months to do.

Everywhere I turned there were critics and judgment, rejection and doubt.

This made me angry. To have my own friends who knew at least a little of what I'd been struggling with and liked my artwork, question my abilities and choices, it hit a raw spot.

After over six years in bed, I didn't feel a lot of self-worth or confidence. I didn't know anything about the art world or how to run a business. I was socially inept because I had been hidden away from the world for so long and still had severe anxiety.

What right did I have to say I was an artist or try to turn it into a business?

How could I possibly do this, especially since I was still nowhere near healthy?

Of course I began to question everything, but I didn't have a ton of choice here, it was either do this, or do nothing. I couldn't get a job, I was still too sick and my "good" time was (and still is) incredibly inconsistent. I have weeks, sometimes months where I can't work due to health problems. I needed something I could do in my own time, on my own schedule, at home from my bed and couch, or some days not at all.

Why not use the sudden drawing skills I'd discovered?

I knew not long after I started drawing that I had something special.

At first I didn't know if my artwork was any good. I had never drawn before and I was locked in a migraine-induced haze in a darkened room. Only my family saw the first pieces of artwork and of course they were going to say they were good, they weren't about to tell a chronically ill, suicidal person that the only thing they've been physically able to do in the last two years was ugly...

So I threw a few images up on Facebook to see what other people thought and there was an incredible response.

I had something. I knew deep down that I had something.

Now I had to figure out how to turn it into a business despite my limitations.

So when friends and strangers alike kept questioning my abilities, my choices, and my efforts to do what I thought was right for me, I either ignored them or quickly stated that it was my life, my decisions.

Your life, your rules.

Always remember that: your life, your rules.

At the end of the day, no one knows your abilities, your dreams, what drives you, or what's important to you, like you do. No one else can see the whole picture that is you. DO NOT let them dampen your spirits or aspirations just because they don't understand. Stand up and go do what you were made to do, no matter what other people might say.

When people doubt you, don't let it sink in. Deflect it and move on.

Know your worth.

Stand up for yourself and your dreams.

Don't back down just because someone else thinks you should. They're speaking from their own limited experience and it has nothing to do with you.

Let's be honest, it might not work out. You might fail. You might struggle and realize later on that you want to move onto something different.

It doesn't matter. You need to do what you feel is right in each moment. That's all you can ask of yourself in this life.

Just do what you feel is RIGHT in each present moment.

If you end up being wrong, learn from your mistake and move on. There's nothing gained by regrets or dwelling on something in the past.

All of this doesn't mean that sometimes you might not be well informed. There might be a subject that comes up in conversation and you don't know anything about it, and therefore your opinion actually could be less valid.

But YOU are not. YOU are valid. YOU are worthy.

Don't forget it's okay to say you don't know. How else are you going to learn? And it's okay to feel like you're the least experienced person in the room. If that's the case, try not to get down on yourself, instead you should congratulate yourself for pushing outside your comfort zone and being willing to learn new things. Being in a room with people who are smarter or more talented than you in some way is the absolute best way to grow as a person.

You, my friend, are a rock star.

7
General Tips

Sometimes you just want a list of things that can help you out, some tips and tricks of the trade to reference and come back to whenever you're feeling down on yourself or anxious, etc.

Well, here is the chapter for that. Below are some general tips, ones that don't necessarily need a whole chapter to themselves to be explained, which can help you when you're struggling with self-doubt, anxiety, and low confidence.

Give Yourself Pep Talks. This one sounds a little weird, but before I do anything that's making me anxious or causing me stress, I talk myself up in my head. This involves a lot of positive self-talk and telling myself that I'm not scared, I'm excited. My body is alert and ready. I am strong and capable. I can do this. Hoorah!

Find a Motto. Sometimes it can help to have a phrase you can easily chant in your mind, or out loud if you want, to help you feel better. Ones I like that you can absolutely steal are: "Whatever happens, happens." "My best is all that matters." "I got this." "No matter what, this is good practice." "Comfort zones are overrated."

Do Something You're Good At. Have you ever noticed your confidence level skyrockets when you do something you're good at? Well, you can capitalize on that feeling by doing something you're good at right before doing something new. By doing something you're already good at, your confidence levels rise and they will stay a little higher as you then attempt something new or nerve-wracking.

Don't Dwell on the Past or Future. We who worry are experts at overanalyzing our past mistakes and dwelling on what might happen in the future. Here's my question for you, though: why does it matter? The most important part of your life is the here and now. Why? Because the past is done and you can't change it, meanwhile the future is unknown and not guaranteed. No one said you're even going to wake up tomorrow, so why are you spending so much of your NOW focusing on being nervous about it? The past is in the past, and though you should use past mistakes as lessons and learn from them, you can't spend time dwelling on them because nothing you ever do will change them. So focus on the NOW. The more you can do this, the calmer and more focused you will be overall.

I tend to find that when I'm feeling depressed, I'm focusing on the past, when I'm feeling anxious, I'm focusing on the future, and when I'm feeling calm and content it's because I'm focusing on the present.

Find a Creative Hobby. Creativity is proven to help you focus on the present, calm your nerves, express your emotions in a healthier way, give you a sense of relief and release, and make you more content. So it doesn't matter what it is, whether it's drawing, painting, sculpting, acting, knitting, scrapbooking, sewing, doodling, making soaps, building something, etching, writing, singing, etc. Just try something and don't focus on whether or not you're good at it, do it for the sake of doing it.

Give Yourself Some Quiet Time. It's hard in today's culture to find time to rest and relax and have some quiet. I'm here to tell you it's important you find the time to do this for yourself. Even if it's just five minutes a day where you sit in your car in a parking lot, find the time to either meditate for those few minutes, or try to think of absolutely nothing, or think about the things for which you're grateful. Just make sure it's quiet and uninterrupted. It could be the five minutes before you get out of bed in the morning, or before you fall asleep at night. It could be taking a break from work, locking your office and basking in the quiet for a few. Or it could be locking yourself in a closet so your kids can't find you and taking those five minutes to yourself. Whatever you need to do.

Make Room for Your Priorities. We all have priorities, but sometimes they get pushed aside by things we THINK are a higher priority. For example, work can sometimes dig into our sleep schedule or eating schedule. In reality it's more important that you sleep well and eat well in order for you to function optimally while you're working, but the stress of work and the social pressure makes us forget that. Our families are a high priority, and yet too often work, our devices, and other responsibilities take us away from our families, leaving us precious little time with them.

It's the same with your own health. The healthier you are, the better you'll be for your loved ones, at work, and the better you'll feel, so why does that not rank as the number one priority? It gets pushed aside due to lack of time or energy. So think, what are your most important priorities and are you making time for them? What could you do to reorganize your life a little to spend more time on the things that matter most to you? What would it take?

Power Poses. There's a great TED Talk by Amy Cuddy that talks about this subject. Power poses are the poses where your back is straight and you're standing tall and your chest is open. One of them is the "Superman" pose where you stand tall and have your hands on your hips. This is the opposite of when you're feeling stressed and scared, which makes you want to close your shoulders and chest forward and hunch or curl up.

What Amy Cuddy says is that when you're confident, you are more likely to be upright and open, with your shoulders back because your emotional state helps dictate your body language. HOWEVER, it can also work the other way. If you aren't feeling very confident but then you strike a power pose for a few minutes, it can help you feel more confident just by being in that pose! It actually decreases your cortisol levels – your fight or flight hormone – and increases your testosterone (confidence). I strike a power pose, usually standing with my hands on my hips, back and shoulders straight before every speech or workshop or event I host.

I even do this when I'm alone at home about to tackle a particularly challenging project because I can feel it help me gain mental clarity and decrease my stress.

Ways to Decrease Nausea. If you're anything like me, when you get exceptionally nervous you might get a little nauseated. Don't worry, that's normal. There are athletes and musicians who throw up before each game or performance they have. It's certainly not pleasant, though! I gave multiple speeches when I was pregnant and I was still in the first trimester full of nausea and fatigue and lightheadedness when I gave my TEDx Talk. These tips below helped get me through.

Things that help some people are: bananas, strong peppermints (This one works best for me, I carry them everywhere! It HAS to be peppermint though, not any other type of mint. Also helpful sometimes if you're feeling sinus congestion.), ginger (works best if you have it regularly), lemon water, popsicles or something cold, eating something small every few hours so your blood sugar doesn't drop, crackers, antacids like Tums, and fresh air.

Give Yourself Some Recognition. Sometimes we're so caught up in what we're doing and where we're going and how far we still have to go that we forget to celebrate our little successes. It's important to recognize the progress you're making and the things you've accomplished, big or small. Have you been nominated for something, made a sale, given a speech, taught a workshop, gotten a new job or promotion, or even just gotten through a whole day without crying/panic attack/etc? Good for you. Recognize your accomplishment before moving on to the next thing.

The other day, despite suffering from a sinus infection and struggling to take care of my son all week when I felt like I just wanted to lie down, I chopped a sweet potato into strips and made sweet potato fries in the oven. They came out better than I expected. Not a big deal but with my sinus infection I felt like I hadn't accomplished anything all week so when my partner got home I was like, "LOOK AT THIS AWESOME THING I DID." I do this a lot because I'm home alone a lot of the time and I know how important it is to voice your successes, big or small, and get recognition and celebrate. I tend to react the same whether it's cooking sweet potato fries or publishing a book or making a big sale: LOOK AT THIS AWESOME THING I DID. I celebrate it all, big and small.

Get Outside. Again, fresh air and nature have been proven to be a huge help in keeping you calm, lowering anxiety, helping you sleep better by regulating your circadian rhythm, and increasing your endorphins. All of that means a better, calmer, healthier, and happier you. So get outside!

Go For a Walk. One of the best things for your health, anxiety, endorphins, and overall happiness is exercise. But don't stress, that doesn't mean it has to be strenuous. In fact, one of the best exercises you can do for yourself and for your mood is to simply go for a walk. Take 15-45 minutes a few days a week and take a walk, if you're able. See what it can do for your mood and confidence. Whenever I'm working on a project that's getting to me and I start to feel overwhelmed and emotionally uncomfortable, I go for a walk. No matter what, I always come back with fresher eyes and more confidence to try and figure out how to conquer that project, especially after about 20 minutes of walking. Can't walk? I couldn't for a number of years and used to have a wheelchair that I also couldn't use by myself, so I get it. There are also stretches and other exercises, really any sort of movement, that can have a similar effect. Just move your body any way you can to get that blood flow.

Dress Consciously. What I mean by that is, don't just grab whatever is lying on top of your bureau. Instead, think about what you own that makes you feel good. When I'm at home working, I never look great. Why would I? No one is going to see me (except my partner, poor guy!). But even some days when I'm home I'll make sure to choose leggings and a shirt that actually match and make me feel more put together and more confident, because it rides over into your work and the rest of daily life. The more attractive you feel, the more confident you tend to feel. So wear clothing that is COMFORTABLE, but also FLATTERING and a style you like. It's almost silly how much it can help you feel better.

On that note I have another point to make: **Don't put any stock in what size clothing you wear.** First of all, it doesn't matter. Second of all, it's all out of whack, I have shirts that are a Small and I have shirts that are an X-Large and they fit me the same, so they're not very reliable anyway. The reason I'm talking about it is because I see far too many people, men and women both I might add, buy a shirt or piece of clothing that is a size too small because that's the size they want to be, but then they're self-conscious and uncomfortable in the shirt because it's too tight (or loose if you're the opposite and considered underweight).

Don't do this.

Just don't do it.

Stop committing these small mistakes that make you feel worse about yourself because they add up and peck at your self-confidence like a little obnoxious woodpecker.

It's not about the size on the tag, which no one will see anyway, it's about how it looks and feels on you. You'll look and feel better if you just get whatever fits you the best, no matter what the size says. Some of you reading this might think this is odd, but I see this happen all the time and for some of you, this is a big adjustment you need to make to help yourself feel less self-doubt.

The tag is hidden, no one will see it. STOP paying attention to it and please pretend it's not there. Pretend sizes don't exist and you then base your decision on ONLY how the article of clothing fits you.

The Week, Month, Year Test. One thing I've discovered that's helped tremendously with my anxiety or anger or sadness or frustration about something is the Week, Month, Year Test. Let's say your significant other does something that bothers you. We all know it's good to pick your battles in a relationship and let some of the lesser things slide, but it's also important to be open and communicative about the things that really bother you so they don't fester and make you start resenting one another down the road. How do you choose which times to speak up? This is a great time to use the Week, Month, Year Test. Think critically about what's

40

bothering you and then ask yourself, will this still bother me in a week? How about a month? What about a year from now? In a year, will you even remember what's happening right now? This can work for events you're nervous about, some of your social anxiety, if something happens that's frustrating, etc. For example, let's say you have a day where a lot of little things have gone wrong and finally to top it all off, you burn your dinner. It's gotten to the point where you cry out of frustration, which is fine, but then start thinking: how important is this moment? Will this still bother me in a week, month, or year? Perhaps it's not as bad as it seems at that moment.

8
Not Everything is a Crisis

It's important to realize something: your anxiety and depression and self-doubt are going to make things seem worse than they really are. It's one of the symptoms! Anxiety can especially make you feel out of control and like every little thing is a crisis.

It's not.

We've all had those days where a million little things have gone wrong and by the end of the day we're falling apart crying on the kitchen floor because we slightly overcooked our dinner. Now, in reality, overcooking dinner is not something we'd typically have a breakdown about, but it's not really about that. It's about all the other little (and big) things that have gone wrong leading up to that moment and our emotional status slowly degrading as the day progressed until it hit this moment, this last little thing to go wrong, and we crumble.

Overcooking your dinner is not a crisis.

I'd bet most of what happened during the day that lead up to that moment wasn't a crisis either.

It's the build-up that wears us down.

So how do we combat that? How do we avoid breaking down or getting panicky over small troubles that keep piling on top of one another?

One way is to simply remind yourself in the moment that it's NOT A CRISIS. Say it to yourself. Say: "This is not a crisis."

If you can train yourself to see each problem by itself instead of a confluence of problems, it can help to minimize their effect on your mental and emotional well-being. Each time something goes wrong, stop and think critically about it. Is this a crisis? Will this still bother me in a week, month, or year? Am I overreacting?

The more you panic and get frustrated, the more likely other things will go wrong too because you're not as focused. A chunk of your attention and energy is being used by your anxiety and frustration and anger, which means you have less left over to do the tasks at hand, which can lead to dropping things, burning things, forgetting things, and doing things wrong.

It's a vicious cycle and it's one you can help stop.

Take a moment to evaluate what is happening and remind yourself of how little importance it really has in your overall life. This one slightly burnt dinner won't stand out a year from now in your memory. You may have shattered a glass on the floor, but it's just a glass.

Depression will make you dwell on the negative things that have already happened.

Anxiety will make you dwell on the negative things that might happen in the future.

Self-doubt makes you dwell on the negative things in the present moment, or at least what your brain has decided you should think is negative, with a mixture of depression and anxiety, past and future.

Dwelling on the negative – whether it's things that have already happened, are currently happening, or could potentially happen in the future – doesn't do you any good. I think we all know that, and yet we continue to do it because our minds have been hijacked by these symptoms. Your depression and anxiety and self-doubt WANT you to dwell because that's how they feed. If you're not focused on the negative, they have nothing to feed off of and they start to lose their power.

So when something bad happens, big or small or somewhere in between, take a moment to stop before you react. Is this a crisis?

Was this caused by me being too anxious and rushing? Was I not focused enough? Is it worth reacting? Will I even remember this in a year?

Stand or sit still for a moment and take a breath deep from your belly and let it out. Slow down. Take stock of your emotions and think about whether or not your initial reaction is an overreaction.

The more things go wrong and the more we dwell on those things, the lower our self-esteem becomes. Suddenly we're thinking we can't do ANYTHING right. We're failures. We're useless. We're burdens on those around us. We're constantly a let-down.

Remember, your self-doubt is feeding off of the negative.

How do we combat that?

Think positive.

Ha. I'm with you if you think that's the most simplistic and unsatisfying answer out there. That's what I certainly thought when people would say it to me and I was so depressed and anxious that I literally could not think straight.

Think positive? Oh…is that all?

Shakes head

It sounds too simplistic. It sounds like someone who's never been through a serious depression just throwing out useless information and lacking the understanding to be at all credible.

Except I've been through it.

Multiple times.

I can tell you with genuine honesty and concern for your mental health, that positive affirmations and focusing on the good things is an effective way to drown out the negative and make sure your self-doubt doesn't have anything to feed upon.

The trouble is how incredibly difficult it is to do in the moment.

Let's remember, your brain has been hijacked! That means in many ways, you've lost control of your emotions and some of your thoughts. When you lose control like that, it's nearly impossible to think positively because every time you try, your self-doubt and depression are going to swat those thoughts away as if they're a pesky fly.

This is why even when you know things like positive affirmations and exercise and socializing will help you feel better emotionally, you can't seem to get yourself to do them. The very things that can help lift you up are also the things you dread and shy away from the most in those darkest moments. Why? Because your depression is in control and it doesn't want you to get better. It wants you to be sedentary and eat bad food to drop your immune system and to dwell on those negative thoughts swirling in your mind.

This is where training your brain comes into play, which is what this whole book is about.

Even on your good days, start practicing some of the techniques in the previous chapter to help not only prevent panic attacks and depressive episodes, but to make yourself more familiar with them and they come more easily to you when you're in the midst of one as well.

The more you focus on the good things and write down or speak about the things for which you're grateful every day, the more it becomes part of your routine and the less hold those negative thoughts have. The more you force yourself to say positive things about yourself, even if you don't currently believe them, the more you're training your brain to see yourself in a better light.

I was having a horrible day a few years ago. It wasn't unusual, being chronically ill, but this one was particularly bad and everything I tried to do turned into a disaster. I had a severe headache and nausea. I tried drawing and felt like I was ruining it. I tried reading and couldn't focus and it made my headache worse. I tried cooking food and burnt the food and myself and spilled things everywhere. I tried watching a movie and the player broke. I looked at my emails and had multiple rejection letters, some of which were not overly pleasant, plus a customer asking where their order was and I realized I hadn't sent it out yet because I forgot. I tripped up the stairs. I spilled on my shirt….

You get it.

Things were building up and I was crying and feeling absolutely horrible about myself. Nothing was going right. I was failing at everything.

So I decided to try going for a walk. It wasn't at all nice out, so I bundled up and started walking around my neighborhood, hunched over, hugging myself and completely wrapped up in my own thoughts.

I was dwelling. I was replaying all the things that had gone wrong that day and my eyes were stinging with tears. My inner monologue was berating me and saying over and over again how much of a failure I was.

The thoughts were swirling, the negativity was building, and I was hugging myself harder, sobbing into the cold breeze. My fingers gripped into my arms, tears rolled down my face, and I was overtaken by misery. I wanted to just collapse.

What use was I? I was a burden and nothing more. What could anyone ever love about me? What importance did my life have?

I can't tell you exactly what happened, but suddenly I felt like I'd been hit in the face with a brick and I stopped walking. I'd been staring at the ground and breathing hard and when I stopped I slowly looked up around me.

No one was there. I was alone in the neighborhood overlooking the hills in the distance and I took a deep breath.

This wasn't helping. This negativity, this constant horrible voice in my head…it wasn't doing me any good!

The reason I stopped in mid-stride was because the brick that hit me was a realization: that voice inside my head was me.

Sure, I knew my inner monologue was me, it was obviously in my own head, but it was at that moment I realized if it was my OWN voice, I should be able to control it better.

That voice in my head was being a bitch. I hate that word and I never use it, but it's apt for this scenario. It was treating me like trash and saying things I would never say to anyone else.

Why was I allowing it to say those things to me?

46

I shouldn't. I didn't deserve it. I hadn't done anything purposefully wrong, I was just having a bad day, and it was time for me to get that voice under control.

I dropped my arms to my sides, clenched my fists and began walking again.

In my head there was a battle raging.

That voice that was so accustomed to dwelling on all the negative things in my life and saying nasty things about me kept taking swings, saying I was a failure, worthless, and a burden. But this time I had another voice, my own REAL voice that would contradict everything she said.

I AM WORTHY.

I AM IMPORTANT.

I AM LOVED.

I AM A GOOD PERSON.

I AM TALENTED.

I AM STRONG.

Slowly, as I kept walking, the first voice started to quiet down. She was my depression and self-doubt and she was losing her power. She was fading because I kept forcing positive thoughts into my mind, yelling them at her in my head, which didn't leave room for the negative ones that fed her.

I AM GRATEFUL FOR MY FAMILY.

I AM GRATEFUL FOR THE ABILITY TO WALK.

I AM GRATEFUL FOR MY TALENTS.

I AM GRATEFUL FOR MY CATS.

It was a fight, but every time the first voice came back with those negative thoughts, I would say NO, and then keep repeating the positive sayings.

I'm a burden. I'm a failu–

NO.

I AM STRONG.

I AM LOVED.

I AM CAPABLE.

Twenty minutes later I was back at my front door. My

head was up. My arms were relaxed by my sides. My breathing was steady. My face was dry. And most importantly, my mind was cleared of the horrible thoughts.

I walked inside and hardly anything went wrong for the rest of the day, and when it did, I moved on quickly without giving it much thought.

There was no more dwelling.

Nothing that happened that day was a crisis and yet my body and mind had put itself in crisis mode, shaking and crying and being completely overwhelmed by misery.

I'd been hijacked.

And then, for the first time, I took back control.

How? By recognizing that the voice in my head was MINE, which meant I could gain control over it with some effort. By forcing positive thoughts to contradict those negative ones, essentially yelling them in my mind to override the negativity.

Those positive thoughts were not easy and it took effort to push them in there and give them ground. Eventually, however, my mind and body started to give more credit to the positive thoughts and pay less attention to the negative, until they faded away, making me feel 10,000 pounds lighter.

I deserved that.

So do you.

9
<u>Guilt</u>

Many of us, especially those of us who deal with self-doubt, carry around a tremendous amount of guilt that weighs us down like a backpack full of bricks. If you were to look inside that backpack, each brick has something written on it, something for which you feel guilty. For example one brick might say "eating unhealthily," another might say "forgot friend's birthday," and another might say "too tired, had to cancel plans," or "didn't get enough work done," or "feeling unmotivated."

Carrying around all these bricks of guilt isn't doing you any good and each brick makes the other bricks feel that much heavier because they pile up. Soon that weight is dragging you down and you're having trouble focusing on anything else.

Remember in the last chapter how we talked about the past, present, and future? The past – which is where a lot of your guilt stems from – is done. It's over and it's never going to change. Dwelling on it won't change it or do you any good.

The best way to make up for something in the past is to do something in the present. For example, you forgot someone's birthday? Make it up to them now. You've been eating unhealthily? Make yourself a plan to try and eat better for the next few days, or just one day a week. There's nothing saying you have to make huge changes right away. It's better for you to take small steps of change.

The past is over and you need to let it go in order to allow your focus to be on the present and what you want right now. Because NOW is the time in your life that matters the most.

Carrying around all that guilt takes a significant amount of energy. That's energy you could be using on, well, anything else! We don't always realize how much energy is being used and wasted on our constant worry, guilt, anxiety, depression, and self-doubt because we've been holding onto it for so long. We've strapped that backpack of guilt tight to our backs and have added to it over time until it's so full it's dragging on the ground.

But why?

What has guilt ever done for you? What good has ever come from it?

Most guilt we carry around isn't worth having at all and it certainly isn't worth keeping and dwelling on it.

A lot of our guilt is driven by our self-doubt. "I'm already overweight, why can't I resist that brownie?" Or, "I'm so tired and not worth it, people will never want to hang out with me."

Guilt is suffocating. I doubt you even realize how much of it you carry around on a daily basis and what it's doing to your energy levels and your self-esteem.

Here's what I want you to do:

Imagine your guilt. All that guilt you carry around is in one big bag.

Now imagine you drag that bag to the edge of a cliff. Thousands of feet below there's a river rushing everything downstream.

Take that bag, haul it up, and push it out over the edge of the cliff. Watch as the bag tumbles in the air and all those bricks of guilt fall out of it and get smaller and smaller as they fall away from you until they finally *splat* into the water of the river and get washed away downstream.

They're out of sight and no longer your problem.

You stand up, straight and tall. Move your shoulders around to feel how much lighter you are now that the weight of that guilt is gone.

Goodbye, guilt.

Breathe deep. You don't need to carry your guilt around and you'll feel immensely better physically and emotionally as soon as you decide to chuck it over that cliff.

For those of us who are chronically ill, this can be especially difficult. When you're sick, injured, tired, have a chronic illness, are suffering from anxiety or depression, are grieving, etc., the guilt can be overwhelming. You feel like a burden on those around you, like you're absolutely no fun to be around, and like you're constantly letting everyone down. You can't function at your optimal levels, which makes you feel like a failure.

However, let's take a minute to analyze this objectively.

I've been chronically ill since 2008, since I was 18, and for the first 6+ years I was undiagnosed and mostly bedridden. I couldn't function. I had a migraine that never left, insomnia so bad I was shaking and hallucinating, and panic attacks that made me mostly unable to leave the house, not that my overwhelming fatigue would let me do that most of the time either…

I felt beyond horrible physically, mentally, and emotionally. I relied on my mom to take care of me and quite literally keep me alive. There was no way I was going to make money or have a job. There was no way I'd be able to go grocery shopping and get myself food. Clean? Socialize? Get a degree? Be productive?

Nope.

I was stuck in this miserable limbo and had no light at the end of the tunnel, very little hope that I would ever get better. I was barely alive.

So what use was I? What purpose did my life have?

I felt SO GUILTY because I was completely dependent on my family and couldn't do a damn thing to help. I certainly wasn't any fun to be around since even talking hurt my head and my brain fog made conversations rather…difficult for the other person to follow at times, to say the least.

My bag of guilt wasn't just on my back; it was a crushing

boulder I couldn't even lift, pinning me down in place.

But here's the thing: What did I really have to feel guilty about?

Guilt implies you did something wrong. If I say something that hurts another person's feelings, I feel guilt because I did something wrong.

That's appropriate.

Getting sick? Being debilitated? Suffering excruciating pain?

I didn't choose to have that happen. I didn't choose to be sick, depressed, or dysfunctional. I didn't choose to be mostly bedridden for years. So why was I being crushed under this guilt? Guilt should only happen if you actually did something wrong, and I didn't.

If you're injured, sick, tired, suffering from depression, anxiety, addiction, someone is bullying you, you're struggling to make ends meet, etc., you don't need to carry around that guilt either. You've been put in a situation where our societal expectations and our expectations of ourselves are too restrictive. Hardly anyone is happy and has lots of energy every day, so why do we beat up on ourselves when we're having a bad day? It's okay. It's normal. Your unnecessary guilt will just make it worse.

So chuck it away. Watch it fall over that cliff and get washed away downstream.

You don't need it.

It's not doing you any good.

Guilt is a form of dwelling and it's another one of those things that can pile up without us realizing what's happening until it's suddenly crushing us.

Try to recognize it. Are you sad, or are you feeling guilty? Why are you feeling down on yourself? Is some of it unnecessary guilt? Is your guilt about something you can control, or something out of your control?

What would happen and how would you feel if that guilt wasn't there?

Visualizing tossing your guilt away helps, but then you have to live it, which is easier said than done, especially because we've trained ourselves to stockpile that guilt and carry it around. This means a shift in your perspective and attitude toward those things making you feel guilty.

This means training yourself, just like in the last two chapters, to push aside those feelings of guilt and replace them with positive or reassuring thoughts. Feeling guilty about being sick or injured? Remind yourself that you didn't choose to be that way, it happens to everyone at one point or another, and it's (usually) temporary. You just have to get through it and those around you are going to have to understand the limitations that come with that situation.

Sometimes explaining your situation can help relieve the feeling of guilt because if people know why you're not available or you're unable to do something, or why you have trouble with something, they'll understand it better and there's less pressure on you. Communicating what's going on can be a huge help. For example, as an artist I do custom commissioned drawings for clients. I never know how my illness is going to be from day to day and sometimes there are months where I don't draw. When I do a commission for someone, they're expecting and hoping for it to be done as soon as possible. I don't blame them, I'd be the same way! So if my illness flairs up and I can't work on it for a while, I start to feel guilty, especially if they start asking about how it's progressing.

How did I combat this problem? I openly communicated about my limitations. Not only do I have it in the contract they sign before I begin that I can't be put on a deadline, and why, I also write to the client to keep them up to date on how things are progressing and if I've had to stop for a while due to illness. So far, everyone has been understanding and I haven't had a single problem or unhappy customer.

All because I addressed the issue upfront and then was open and honest about it as the projects progressed.

So communicate. Get it off your chest (or back) and allow those around you to know what's going on so they can be more understanding too. Lower the amount of pressure on yourself to be everything to everyone.

It's okay to say no.

It's okay to be tired.

It's okay to take a break.

It's okay to need time to yourself.

You're not a bad parent for needing time away from your kids. You're not a bad employee for needing a vacation or a day off or saying no, you can't be put on that strict of a deadline. You're not a bad friend for having to cancel plans. And you're not a bad person for having to say no.

Respect your limitations.

Understand what you need in the moment to help yourself be healthier, happier, and better for tomorrow.

Don't let guilt influence your actions or weigh down your emotions.

Push it off the cliff and move on to the next thing.

10
Making Decisions

Have you ever found that because of your self-doubt and anxiety you have trouble making decisions? Mine used to be so bad I would have a breakdown trying to decide what to wear in the morning and sit on the floor crying with clothing strewn all around me.

Every. Day.

I also couldn't go to a restaurant for a while because I wouldn't be able to decide what to eat and would start to have a panic attack and shake and cry.

It sounds ridiculous to someone who is healthy or hasn't suffered from severe anxiety, but those simple situations suddenly became overwhelming and I was debilitated. It was horrible for me and equally hard on those around me who didn't know how to help or why it was happening.

Decision-making can be a huge trigger for anxiety and self-doubt.

For me, I always had a voice in the back of my head that was still 'sane' during a panic attack telling me how unreasonable my reaction was and how I needed to just pick an outfit or a meal and move on.

That voice, however, wasn't enough. My anxiety had taken over and I was no longer driving the vehicle. I'd been stuffed in the back seat with my anxiety in control, which meant despite still being able to hear that reasonable voice, it couldn't do anything to change the situation. My anxiety was too strong and I was too far gone.

The first step I used to help overcome this problem was to try and prepare in advance. For example, if we were planning to go out to eat, I would look up their menu online and pick my meal before I was in the situation, with a backup just in case that one was unavailable. We started by going to places I'd been before so I would be able to choose something I knew I would like. That way, there wasn't a single decision I would have to make in the moment and it allowed me to relax a little.

Preparing in advance like this helped a great deal, but it was only available for certain situations. Most decisions we make aren't known in advance and we can't have it planned out.

The next step to help me overcome this problem was to flip a coin. I know, this sounds too simple, but if I've narrowed something down where I can't decide between two things, or it's a yes or no situation, and I felt my anxiety rising, I would take out a coin BEFORE my anxiety had total control of the situation and flip it. Heads was one thing and tails was the other. Then, whatever it landed on was my decision.

Now here's the trick with this one: I got so only about half the time I'd actually go with whatever the coin indicated. Why? Because the coin allowed me to realize my real preference. If it came up yes and I felt a sense of relief, then it was the right choice. If it came up yes and I felt disappointed or some dread, perhaps it was the wrong choice. After a while I could start to distinguish how I felt thanks to the coin and it made it easier to make the decision, even if it wasn't what the coin told me to do.

Tougher decisions are, well, tougher. This is where some of our other training from previous chapters starts to come in.

Decision-making is easier when you're calm. When you're calm, you're more rational and clear-headed, which makes it easier to analyze a situation objectively. This is helped by practicing meditation, as that can help you learn to focus your mind, calm your thoughts, and lower your cortisol levels.

Walking can help lower your cortisol levels, ease your anxiety, and get fresh blood flowing to your brain for a clearer head.

(Go to the General Tips chapter for more things that can help you get and maintain your calm, clear your mind, focus, and increase your good hormones while lowering your bad anxiety and depression-inducing hormones.)

The more you practice these tips and techniques we've talked about, the more prepared your brain is going to be for decision-making.

One thing I realized during my time with daily panic attacks was that I eventually could feel them coming. At first, a panic attack felt like it came out of the nowhere because I wasn't used to them and didn't notice the warning signs leading up to the moment when I was overwhelmed and lost control. After a while I realized that before it was a full-blown attack, I would be tense and some of my muscles would twitch, especially in my jaw. I could recognize that the voice in my head was getting faster and repeating itself. My palms might get sweaty and my hands would be shakier. My breathing would be quicker and shallower. I would start fidgeting and my motions would be quick and jerky. I found myself rubbing my forehead or gripping my hair.

These were all warning signs that I was on my way to a panic attack and subsequent loss of control.

Eventually, as I began to recognize these signs, I was able to counteract them, which is something I got better at over time and now I haven't had a full-blown panic attack in a number of years.

If my breathing was becoming quick and shallow, I would slow it down and try to breathe deeper and from my belly. If I was fidgeting, I would try to sit or stand still, or even lie down, and focus on those deep breaths while trying to relax my muscles. I would stretch and breathe and think about something completely different for a few minutes to try and clear the clutter in my brain. I would make some honey-lavender tea, take a hot shower/bath, go for a walk, or distract myself with a funny video.

Then, when I was feeling calmer, I would try to tackle the

decision again.

Once your brain is more relaxed you can focus on the problem at hand and try to let logic prevail. Most decisions are based on logic, so if you can calmly analyze the pros and cons of either side of a decision, it can make it easier.

There's a difference, however, between analyzing and over-analyzing.

Each decision you make shouldn't take much time. It's good to analyze what the outcome and consequences of any decision might be so you can use that knowledge to make the best decision possible, but spend too much time on it and you're dwelling again.

Dwelling, in regards to a decision, means dwelling on the future, which is typically caused by anxiety. It's anxiety that makes decisions so hard. It's not knowing what the outcome will be and that lack of control that makes us uncomfortable.

You're never going to have control over the outcome of a decision and the future. Let it go and do the best you can with the information you have. The more you dwell, the more you're letting your anxiety take over the situation.

You should also know that because of your anxiety and self-doubt, sometimes your "gut" is wrong. I do believe in intuition and think it can help you make decisions …sometimes.

There's something called the "laugh-cry response," which is when a decision you've made makes you elated and also terrified. This is usually with big decisions that could change your day-to-day life, such as quitting your job to become a freelancer, or buying a house, or having kids. This can be a good sign about a decision because it's something that pushes you toward a dream, and it also means you're pushing yourself out of your comfort zone to get there. That takes work and has unknown factors that make it wonderful and terrifying.

Your intuition, however, can get muddled when you're anxious. Your anxiety and self-doubt will cling to your intuition, making it waver and be unclear, which means your gut reaction to something might be skewed or completely inaccurate. Therefore, if you're calm, focused, and clear-headed and your intuition is telling you something about a situation, then it's a good bet there's some truth to it. But if you're anxious and fidgety and your mind is cluttered with doubt, I wouldn't put as much stock in your intuition at that time.

Decisions happen every day. You decide what you're going to wear, what to eat, who to talk to, what work to do, when to do things, how to do things, what to watch on TV, etc. Some of them will have very little consequence and some are major decisions that make you uncomfortable, frightened, and anxious.

Know that everyone makes mistakes.

Everyone hates tough decisions.

No one has control over all the consequences of a decision.

Try to keep yourself calm in order to focus on your decision rationally and objectively. What are the pros and cons? What are the likely potential outcomes and consequences? If you flip a coin to help make the decision, how does the outcome make you feel? If you're calm and collected, what is your intuition telling you? How could this decision affect others? Is there really a right or wrong choice? How important is this decision (think the week, month, year test) in the grand scheme of things?

All you can do is make the decision based on the information you have at that moment. Perhaps that means you need to look for more information, if that's a possibility. Maybe it means asking for opinions from people you respect.

Just know the difference between analyzing and dwelling, being anxious and being focused.

No matter what, you're going to have to make this decision, so do it as efficiently and calmly as you can for the best results. Then, as I've said many times, move on to the next thing. When it's done, it's done. Try not to dwell.

11
The Comfort Zone

It might seem like if you suffer from anxiety and self-doubt, you should stay inside your comfort zone. When you do things you're already good at, you have more confidence, right? Logic would suggest that if you stay within that zone and focus on just the things you're good at, your confidence should be higher and your self-doubt should be lower.

In the real world, however, this doesn't seem to ring true.

Unfortunately, you can't grow – as a person, business, in your job, in relationships – or get better at anything if you don't push yourself outside your comfort zone.

The best opportunities that come your way are only going to happen if you're not camped out inside your comfort zone.

But let's face it, it's called the comfort zone for a reason and those of us with self-doubt and anxiety are petrified of leaving it. We walk over to the edge to try and it feels like there's a bungee cord pulling us back. Even when we WANT to leave the comfort zone and try something new, anxiety or panic attacks or self-doubt and our jerk of an inner monologue can prevent us from being able to accomplish this goal. Then it fills us with even MORE self-doubt and guilt for not being able to do it.

It's okay to be scared. Trust me when I say, it's still worth it.

I'm petrified every day of my life. Let's remember I used to have panic attacks so badly I couldn't even get groceries or drop off artwork at a gallery. I used to get panic attacks at home, doing absolutely nothing! That meant I was going outside my comfort zone for pretty much…everything.

I had no comfort zone.

It was terrible.

Skip forward to today and I run my own business, give speeches, teach workshops, do consulting for other artists, etc. Every time it's out of my comfort zone. And every time it gets a little easier.

Your comfort zone is overrated.

If you stay within your comfort zone, not only will you not grow as a person, you'll be feeding your self-doubt and lack of confidence. Every time an opportunity comes your way, you'll have to turn it down and feel worse about yourself.

No risk, no reward.

Think about exercise. If you do one type of exercise, it starts out challenging and then gets easier the more you do it. Then your body is comfortable with it. Eventually your body is too comfortable and if you do the exact same amount of exercise in the exact same way, it doesn't have the same benefits or effects as it used to. If you were to switch it up, though, by doing a different exercise or doing your initial exercise for longer or harder, you'd notice a difference again. It would be more challenging, but your body would respond and it would benefit you more.

Good things will happen when you venture outside your comfort zone, but that doesn't mean you need to go skydiving or give a huge presentation right away.

When you're exercising, it's best to increase your time or weight or whatever it is by small amounts rather than trying to change things drastically. With weightlifting, you start out at a weight that you can do, but is a challenge. You stay there for a little while until it's comfortable and then you add a little weight, just enough to make it a challenge again but not too difficult where you'll strain yourself. Again, you're there for a little while until it's comfortable and then you add more weight.

This is how you should approach leaving your comfort zone

too, especially if you suffer from self-doubt or anxiety – in small steps.

For example, if you're thinking about public speaking, start with a short speech to a small group about something you know very well. The topic should be within your comfort zone, it's that action of speaking about it in front of a group of people that will be your new challenge. Do this a few times to get a little more comfortable before you try speaking on a different topic or to a larger group.

The more you do something, the more knowledge and experience you'll have, and the more confidence you'll gain. We talked about that in previous chapters about Practice and Knowledge Gains Confidence.

Eventually, what was once outside your comfort zone will slowly be brought within your comfort zone, or at least much closer to it.

You don't need to leap outside your comfort zone to make progress and grow and gain confidence, you just need to step outside it on a regular basis. Even baby steps.

This isn't something where you do it once and suddenly you have confidence and your self-doubt has disappeared. You need to do it continually and make it a practice.

The more you step outside your comfort zone, the more confidence you'll have to keep stepping outside it and try new things.

It's scary, but it's worth it.

This doesn't mean you're not going to fail. Trying anything new raises your risk of failure, hence the reason we shy away from it. That's why smaller steps are key. If you tried to add 100 pounds to your weightlifting routine at once, your chance of failure is much higher and more likely than if you add 5 pounds at a time.

This means setting smaller goals that are more achievable and allowing yourself to work toward something gradually instead of needing to be good at it right away. Focus on and celebrate each small achievement and allow them to add up and build your confidence as you move forward. Don't expect miracles. Don't expect things to happen overnight. You are a constant work in progress and you have all the time in the world to keep challenging yourself and growing into the person you want to be.

There's no rush.

If you take steps regularly to grow your comfort zone a little at a time in your job, relationships, hobbies, business, personal character, and more, you'll start seeing a change in your confidence levels as well.

The more you've done, the more experience you have, the more challenges you've overcome, and the more knowledge you have gained, the more confidence you'll build.

12
Socialize

For some of us with self-doubt, depression, and/or anxiety, socializing can be one of the most terrifying and dreaded experiences out there.

People? Why? Why would I want to be around people when I could be snuggled up at home with a fuzzy blanket and my cat?

This can be especially true if it's a situation that involves people we don't know, like a networking event, party, fundraiser, etc. Then the urge to crawl under something and hide can become even stronger.

You may dread it, but it's necessary.

Loneliness breeds self-doubt. Why do you think so many artists who work alone in their studios have such overwhelming self-doubt? Part of it comes from a lack of socialization.

Relationships are important, and I don't just mean your immediate family, although they are certainly important. You need all kinds of relationships, from family and close friends to acquaintances and coworkers and that person whose name you can never remember.

Why? Because it takes different types of socialization to have each of those levels of relationship and they can all help you.

We may not feel like it, but humans are social beings. It's in our DNA to seek out the company of other people. So when we deny that part of us, it can cause problems. Typically, those problems show up as depression, anxiety, and self-doubt.

Now if you're like me, one of the biggest triggers for my anxiety is socializing, aptly called "social anxiety." This means going out and talking to people scares me. Even when it's people I know, socializing can be very uncomfortable for me and I can get withdrawn. I don't mean to, it just happens. Or I have so much anxiety leading up to it that I show up all jittery and awkward or end up canceling my plans.

That's okay. You need to know your limitations and keep those in check. Sometimes you can't do it.

Just don't let yourself be complacent.

You need to socialize!

Socializing and relationships are important for your mental health and emotional wellbeing. Plus, the only way you're going to find the people who speak to your soul, those with whom you can be comfortable no matter what and bring out the best in you, is to go out and look for them.

I felt misunderstood for most of my life. Now I understand some of that was having depression from a very young age without realizing it, but part of it was also my lack of socializing. I grew up thinking I didn't like people, but now I can see it wasn't that I didn't like them, it was a mixture of social anxiety and not having found the RIGHT people for me. Once you find those people, socializing becomes something completely different and it can help you feel more whole as a person.

Even when you're not fully feeling it, try to socialize anyway. You've made plans and as they approach you start dreading going out. That's okay, but make an effort to do it anyway. It's likely it will make you feel better, not worse, especially if it's with your friends who make you laugh.

Socializing for some people can be like this: 1.) You dread going out. 2.) You go out and end up having a great time and immediately make plans to do it again. 3.) Despite your initial excitement, as new plans approach, you dread going out again.

I'm not sure what causes us to dread something even when we had a great time the last time, but it happens. It's a cycle that happens again and again. See if you can try to skip the last step and keep reminding yourself how much fun you had last time to help motivate you, or at least have it stop you from canceling.

Another part of socializing that people with self-doubt struggle with is: compliments.

Learn to take a compliment.

It's awkward. You don't feel great about yourself so when someone says something nice about you, your brain immediately tries to bat it down with negativity.

Stop doing that and go read the chapter about your inner monologue.

Don't let that negative voice in your head (that is constantly telling you how bad everything is) come out of your mouth. Ideally, you should start to try and kick it out of your head too, but even if you haven't done that yet, don't let it slip between those lips.

When someone says you look nice or you're good at something or any other type of (non-creepy) compliment, smile and say thank you. Appreciate the fact that this person didn't have to say it to you. They took the time and energy to notice something about you and then speak to you in a kind way. That's awesome and they deserve more in return than you trying to contradict them.

Plus, you deserve to revel in the compliment, no matter what that negative voice is saying inside your head.

Self-doubt can make it difficult to hear positive things about yourself, but you should know and recognize that it's nonsense. Everyone has positive things about themselves and they deserve to be complimented on those things. Plus the person who is complimenting you has an opinion they're sharing and it's not your job to invalidate that opinion.

Even if you don't agree with the compliment, accept the good energy and kindness that comes with it.

While we're talking about compliments, another great thing to learn to do while you're out and about socializing is to GIVE compliments to others. Not only is it a nice thing to do, there's a ton of research that shows you can make yourself happier by making

66

others happier. So if you do something nice for someone, like pay them a compliment, it will make you feel better too. Not to mention, you never know what someone else is going through. Perhaps they're grieving or suffering from depression or self-doubt themselves and they do a good job of hiding it when they're in public. Your words could mean a lot to them. Your words could help brighten their day or week or month. Your kind words might be exactly what they needed in that moment.

So don't be sparing with your own compliments. The world needs more people freely handing out kind words to one another.

13
A Chapter for Creatives

My other two books are aimed at artists and creatives and even though this book is for a more diverse audience, self-doubt is an issue that plagues almost every artist and crafter I know in one way or another. This issue is extremely prevalent in the creative world.

What I find particularly interesting is that there's a lot of research that shows having a creative hobby, like scrapbooking, painting, knitting, or any other creative task, is something that can help increase your happiness levels. So then why are so many creatives, people who do these things all the time, suffering from depression?

I have a few theories, but you should recognize that's what they are – theories. I don't have scientific studies to point to that show why creatives are more likely to feel this way. However, as I talked about before, isolation can be a key factor. A lot of creatives spend a significant amount of time alone in their studios, isolated from the rest of the world, and they might lack the proper amount of socialization for their emotional well-being.

Artists also pour a lot of themselves into their creative work, which can be draining when you do it all the time, as opposed to having a hobby you can do whenever you'd like. When it's a hobby I think the person tends to pour out just enough of themselves to feel better, pouring out the bad energy as they focus on their creation, turning it into something good, distracting themselves from their worries. When you do creative work more and more often, it's different and you end up pouring out not just the bad energy, but some of the good as well. It can still be beneficial for you and make you feel better, but there's only so much energy in your system to be poured out into your creations.

Another aspect is social and financial pressure. As a hobby, you don't have to worry about where this particular painting is going to be displayed, if it will sell, if anyone will like it, or feel like you have to finish it within a certain deadline. You're doing it specifically for you, which means even if it never gets finished, there's no pressure. Whereas an artist needs to keep putting out new work to satisfy their audience, is worried if people will like it, if it will sell, how much to charge for it, how to promote it, where to display/sell it, and when it will get done. Some of the joy has been stripped away simply because of all the pressure put on us by our community and ourselves.

Perhaps it makes sense, therefore, that even though a creative hobby can help raise happiness levels and emotional well-being, being a creative who sells their work and would like to make a living or part of a living off their work can have a different, more negative effect.

So now that we realize creatives may have a harder time with this, let's talk about some ways you can help boost your creative confidence and crush the self-doubt that surrounds you and your work.

First thing is first – What do you call yourself?

I don't mean your name or even your business name, I mean when someone asks you what you do, are you comfortable saying you're an artist? Can you say with confidence and no hesitation "I'm an artist," or "I'm a musician," or whatever your creative craft is?

This sounds easy but it can take artists a long time to be able to say this with confidence. It took me a long time. I didn't say it with confidence until well after I'd had exhibits and newspaper articles about me and had sold thousands of dollars worth of product.

Why? What makes it catch in our throats when we try to say

it?

Part of it is our self-doubt. Am I a REAL artist? Do I have the right to call myself an artist?

Let's just be clear: yes, you are a real artist.

What does that even mean? What qualifies someone to be a "real" artist? A certain amount of money made? A certain amount of work created?

I don't think so.

Everyone is an artist in one way or another. We were all born artists. We were all born creative.

If you think you're not a PROFESSIONAL artist, all you have to do is ask yourself this one question: have you ever sold anything related to your creative work?

It doesn't matter if the only thing you've sold is a 50 cent sticker, if you've sold ANYTHING related to your creative work, you are considered a professional.

The definition of professional is whether or not you've ever made money from something. Therefore, even that 50 cent sticker or $4 greeting card knocks you up from the amateur level to the professional level.

So, have you sold anything? If so, welcome to the club of people who can call themselves professional artists!

If you haven't sold anything, that's fine too! When you do you can call yourself a professional, and until then, you're still an artist! You create, right? Then welcome to the club of people who can call themselves artists!

Another reason we might shy away from saying we're an artist with confidence is that we're not sure how the other person is going to react. I find most of the time there tends to be two types of reaction, which I'll explain below.

The first type is the person who either shrugs you off or asks what you really do or what your real job is, etc. These people have absolutely no idea how difficult it is to be a creative and perhaps think we just sit at an easel painting "happy little trees" every day with not a care in the world.

They're not your people.

We can try to gently educate those people, but in general, they're not your people.

The second type is the person who starts asking more questions about what you do and gets excited about it. These people tend to either be other artists and are showing interest because they know what it's like and love creativity, or they're people who don't necessarily do it themselves but are in awe of those who can. These are your people! This is your audience. These are the people who are more likely to buy from you, remember you, talk about you to friends, etc. Always give these people your business card or some way to follow your work and reach out to you.

No matter whom you're talking with, I give you permission to say with confidence that you're an artist.

Even if you have a day job that's completely unrelated, I don't care. Feel free to talk about that too, and then mention your side-hustle or other business or whatever you want to call it that is your creative work.

The more confidence you show, the more seriously people are going to take you. Trust me, I hardly ever get asked what my "real" job is anymore because I'm confident and professional when I tell them about myself as an artist, hand them my business card, and explain what I do.

"I'm a wildlife artist as well as an author and speaker. Here's my business card where you can see a couple thumbnail examples of my colored pencil artwork…"

Boom.

That's it.

At that point if they're at all interested in my work or me, they'll start asking questions, usually prompted by seeing the examples of my work and wondering how on earth I got colored pencil to look like THAT. (If you're wondering what I mean by that, feel free to check out my artwork here: www.corrinathurston.com)

Try it. The next time someone asks you that typical question about what you do, try and answer it without hesitation. It's just a

71

conversation, but you deserve to acknowledge your skills. Say it like you would say, "I'm a doctor," if you were one.

You are an artist.

As an artist, I want you to pledge to yourself right now that you will treat yourself as a professional. There's a difference between a hobby and a job, even if that job is only very, very part time. If you're trying to sell your work or get booked at venues, or gain clients in some way, then what you're doing is a job. It should be treated that way.

This means presentation matters.

Have business cards. Do your bookkeeping. Speak and dress in a professional manner when you're representing your business. Be clear and concise. Market yourself and your work to reach your current and new audiences. Push yourself to discover new opportunities for your work.

Also, especially in the creative world, expect and accept rejection. It's going to happen. Regularly.

I get rejected all the time. I get ignored. I get negative comments.

It doesn't matter.

Art and writing and anything creative is incredibly subjective. Some people are going to love what you do and rave about it. Some people are going to call it trash or brush you aside with disinterest.

Don't worry about it.

I know it's easier said than done, but honestly, it's not worth the time or effort. Any energy you spend on negative people or any rejections you take personally is energy you could be spending on something else, something better.

Rejection is great.

Rejection means you are pushing yourself outside your comfort zone and striving to find new opportunities for yourself and your work. There's a whole chapter in my first book, **How To Build Your Art Business with Limited Time or Energy,** that focuses on rejection, and one part that I'll talk about here too is the definition, which is why you shouldn't put too much stock in it or dwell on it.

This is my definition: *"Rejection happens when what you're offering isn't QUITE what the other person is looking for."*

That's it.

That's all it is.

Perhaps the gallery you approached has already displayed a lot of work like yours and they are trying to diversify. It's not necessarily that they don't like your work. Or perhaps it's the opposite and they typically take a very specific style of artwork and don't feel yours is quite in line with that style.

Maybe you send a proposal to a retailer but unbeknownst to you, they are full and not accepting any new work right now. They might not tell you that in the rejection, or they might not get back to you at all.

So don't fret when you get rejected. It's going to happen. Often. And it's absolutely NOT a reason to get down on yourself.

Need some inspiration? Take a look at this list:

- Walt Disney was fired from a job because he "lacked imagination."
- Oprah was fired from her job as a news reporter.
- Lucille Ball was told to try another profession and give up on acting before her role on I Love Lucy.
- Stephen King's first book was rejected thirty times.
- Likewise, Dr. Seuss's first children's book was rejected many times before finally finding a publisher that would take a chance on it.
- In high school, Michael Jordan was cut from the basketball team.
- Meryl Streep was told she was "too ugly" to be a leading actress.

Rejection happens to everyone, especially when in the creative world because of how subjective it is. Plus, the art world in general is overly critical, and competition is fierce.

What this means is, even if you keep getting rejected,

don't let it stifle you with self-doubt and don't let it stop you from continuing to put yourself out there. Each rejection, each failure, each misstep is getting you that much closer to your next opportunity and success.

Success doesn't happen without failures and rejection. So try to take it in stride and push past it.

Another trap creatives fall into is comparing yourself and your work to that of other people. You should definitely look at and support other artists' work, as we're a community. Artists need to help and support other artists. Looking at other artists' work and success can also be incredibly inspiring and help you burst out of a creative drought.

Unfortunately, the opposite is true as well. Sometimes when you see another artist's work you start to feel bad about your own because you think theirs is so much better. Or you wonder how another artist is having so much success and start to feel bad about yourself for not achieving as much as they have.

Their artwork and their success have nothing to do with you, or you with it. Not to mention, they feel the same way about other people who are more successful than them and might view your artwork as better than theirs. It's all subjective, remember? Plus, that artist might seem more successful than they really are. Just because someone has had a lot of press and articles about them and you've noticed their name in a bunch of different locations doesn't mean it's always translating into sales and income.

Sometimes looks can be deceiving.

Still, no matter what, there's no point in comparing yourself and your work to anyone else. There's no point thinking you're better than other people, and there's no point thinking you're worse than other people, because it doesn't matter when it comes to you and your work.

The only thing that matters is you're continuing to grow and do the best you can to try and accomplish your goals, whatever those may be. Only compare yourself to your past self. How are you doing? How could you do things better or more efficiently or grow your skill set?

To add on to this, know that your work – no matter what anyone else thinks – is always good enough. Everyone has their own style, their own interpretation, and their own creative journey. Even if you're just starting out, your work is good enough. True, it might and should get better over time, your talent will become more precise as you hone your craft, but that doesn't mean what you can do right now isn't good or interesting.

As an artist, your creative work is about you. You don't need to create something because you think other people will like it, create what YOU like, and your interest and passion will show through. Then you can focus on finding the right people for that particular piece because they're out there somewhere. You don't have to conform or change how you create. Your creative work is a part of you, which is why it can be hard to put it out there, hear negative comments, or get those rejections. If it weren't a part of us, if we hadn't poured part of ourselves into it, we wouldn't care.

It takes practice and discipline to shield us from the negative emotions that can come with those things and the self-doubt they can produce.

You are an artist.

You will be rejected, and that's normal and fine.

You will get negative comments, and that's normal and fine too.

Your work is always good enough.

There's no need to compare yourself to anyone else, ever.

You are a professional. The sooner you believe that and start taking action – like buying business cards, having an online presence, learning to market your work better, and having a good presentation of your work – the sooner you'll start feeling more confident about it and the less your creative self-doubt will rear its ugly head.

Don't forget to check out my other two books!
How To Build Your Art Business with Limited Time or

14
Ways to Reduce Stress

We all know too much stress can be toxic and wear us down. I say too much because some amount of stress is actually good for you. There are two different types of stress: eustress, which is good stress, and distress, which is bad stress.

Good stress is when you are nervous but excited about a project you're working on or a presentation you're going to give or an upcoming interview. It's still stressful, but it's a good thing that's causing it and it can help fire you up.

Bad stress is where your loved one is sick or your job is putting too much pressure on you with unrealistic deadlines or you're having trouble communicating in your relationship and it's causing arguments. This is the type of stress that just wears you down and is bad for your health.

For this chapter, we're focusing on how to manage and help eliminate the effects of bad stress in your life.

Why talk about stress? Because stress can be a factor in your self-doubt. The more overwhelmed you feel, the more things go wrong, the more you have to worry about, the less happy, healthy, and confident you're going to feel. That stress is going to eat away at your self-esteem.

So here are some tips and techniques to help manage the symptoms and decrease the effect it'll have on your health, mood, and confidence.

Not My Circus, Not My Monkeys. I saw this phrase online one time and I've used it ever since. What it means is: if there are people around you who are stressed or overwhelmed and you're the type of person who tends to suck that energy up like a sponge, you don't have to. Say your coworker is having a terrible day and they are constantly complaining and overwhelmed and you find your own mood dropping. Tell yourself: "Not my circus, not my monkeys." As in, this is not your stress so you don't need to hold onto it. Maybe people nearby are arguing and the whole place is getting tense because of their stress: "Not my circus, not my monkeys."

This doesn't mean you shouldn't try to help someone in need or stand up for someone who is getting bullied, etc. It just means you need to evaluate a situation that's causing you stress and decide, is this really my stress? Do I need to be spending energy and attention on this stress, or is it something that person is going to have to figure out on their own and I shouldn't be worrying about it?

Become a Screen Door. Similarly, you can learn to let the stress of others wash through you and have less effect on your own mood. For example, you've had a decent day and you're cooking dinner and someone else in your household comes home in a terrible mood. They slam the door and barely speak to you, or they vent to you and they forget to appreciate the fact that you're cooking dinner for them or don't even ask about your day because they are so caught up in their own stress.

This can immediately cause you to tense and feel like you've had a bad day too. Your mood plummets because you're soaking up their aura of stress and on top of that you're a little upset that they're so caught up in themselves so as to barely acknowledge your efforts or ask about your day. Suddenly your decent day has been overtaken by this whirlwind of negativity and you're feeling tense, frustrated, sad for them, sad for you, etc. Your decent day and mood have unraveled in an instant.

But why?

Yes, you should feel bad for them, it's called empathy. You know what it's like to have a horrible day and feel that kind of stress, so you can understand how they feel, and it's valid. They have a right to feel that way, but they don't have a right to take it out on you, and you don't need to fall to the same level of misery as them. You can still feel badly for them and try to comfort them without letting your own mood plummet.

How?

Learn to become a screen door.

I know that sounds weird, but hear me out. Visualize a screen door as the wind comes up around it. That screen door can absolutely feel that wind flying through the door and if it wasn't latched, it would swing that door around, but it's also letting the majority of the wind go right through it.

You're the screen door and the stress of other people is the wind.

Yes, you can feel it and it can initially hit you hard, but then, if you focus, you can let most of that stress blow through you by remembering it's not YOURS.

This isn't your stress. You don't need to capture it all and try to hold onto it. Instead, you can walk through it and let it wash past you.

The dinner scenario I wrote about above is what happened to me the first time I really understood and utilized this technique. My mood plummeted and what I thought was a good day turned sour in an instant. But then I thought, why? Why am I letting my entire day and good mood get disrupted this much by something that doesn't really have anything to do with me? There was no reason my mood had to get squashed, I was letting that happen by accepting all that bad energy into myself instead of letting most of it blow through.

Now one of the reasons I chose a screen door instead of a shield or full door is because if you teach yourself to block out the emotions of other people entirely, you'll lose your empathy. You can get too good at ignoring the emotions of those around you and then you're unable to connect or comfort them and you lose your ability to care. We don't want that, we just want you to be able to be around the stress of other people without succumbing to that stress yourself.

The screen door doesn't block all the stress; it feels all of it and then lets it through. You can acknowledge that stress and how that other person is feeling and understand where they're coming from without having to be miserable too.

Once I realized this and implemented it, I instantly felt lighter. Yes, a loved one had a horrible day and was stressing and full of negativity at the moment, but that negativity didn't have to fill me too. I had had a good day. I didn't have to let go of that good energy just because it contradicted the energy of those around me, in fact it could potentially help them feel better too.

Meditation. We've talked about this before, but meditation can help you relieve stress by helping get more oxygen to your brain, helping you focus, and calming your nerves. I particularly like active meditation, which is where you focus on your breathing while you're doing something else, like walking, yoga, driving, etc. For me, walking is the best because a walk is proven to significantly help reduce anxiety and is one of my go-to remedies for an impending panic attack or high anxiety day. To add on the meditative aspect of focusing on your breathing and breathing from your belly, just makes it that much more effective. But regular meditation is great too. All you have to do is sit or stand or lie down and quietly focus on your breathing. This could mean counting your breaths, or breathing in for a certain number of beats and breathing out for a certain (usually longer out) number of beats, or visualizing your breath as the rise and fall of a wave or pendulum, etc. Anything that keeps your focus on your breath and allows you to breathe from your belly is good.

Yoga/Stretching. Stress can accumulate in your muscles. Have you ever noticed when you're stressed or anxious, your muscles feel tight? My sciatica will act up and my muscles will be very tight on a bad day. This means taking the time to stretch the muscles can be a huge benefit.

When your muscles are tight they tend to capture and hold toxins and your blood flow is limited. This means not as much blood is going to each of those muscles or your brain. There are different types of stretching, both of which are good for you. There's static stretching and dynamic stretching. There's nothing wrong with either, but the dynamic stretching will be more beneficial because you're both stretching and using/strengthening the muscles at the same time. For example, sitting on the floor with your legs straight out and leaning forward to stretch your hamstrings is a relatively static stretch because you're stretching the muscle without using it much. A lunge, on the other hand, is a dynamic stretch because you are stretching the same muscles while also using/engaging them.

When your muscles are looser and more relaxed, so is your body, helping to relieve that stress you've been holding. The blood flow is helping release those toxins and clear your head, which also decreases the effects of stress.

Writing. There's a peculiar energy associated with writing. Have you ever had a problem or been dwelling about something and then when you wrote it down you felt at least a little better? This is especially true if you write it by hand, but writing it on a computer helps too.

What is that? What makes writing something out so beneficial?

My guess is that when you write or draw or create anything, you're using a specific type of energy and releasing it onto the paper. It's a physical and emotional release I don't fully understand, but I know it can work.

Some people even take it a step further and burn the paper afterwards. For example, you're dwelling over some stressor in your life, like your parents getting a divorce, so you take out a piece of lined paper and start writing about it. You write about your role in the divorce and how it's making you feel being put in the middle of your two parents, how they're behaving, how frustrated you are, etc. Then, once you're done writing, you take a match or a lighter and your paper over to a sink or somewhere that you won't catch anything on fire (somewhere safe) and you light the corner of the paper. Then you just watch it burn. The paper, your words, and all that negative, stressful energy you poured into it, will burn and transform into ash and smoke that drifts away.

Increase the positive, decrease the negative. Sometimes without realizing it, we fill our lives with too much negativity and not enough positivity. You can easily add more positivity to your life via things like: funny videos, reading, telling jokes, being around funny/happy people, remembering the best times you've had, looking around and finding the beauty in your life and noticing all the things for which you're grateful, pets, positive news stories, etc. Plus, you can try to decrease the negativity around you as well. Things like: too much negative news, remove toxic people from your life or at least limit them, avoid things that make you feel bad about yourself like beauty magazines, certain people, etc.

When you decrease the number of things in your life contributing to the negativity and increase the things creating positivity, it can help rebalance your overall mood and lower your stress.

Avoid Triggers. Similarly, if you can avoid stressful triggers, that can help as well.

We all have those things that instantly trigger us to start stressing. For me, it's certain people, or driving somewhere I've never been, or lots of traffic, or doing something new in front of people. I try to limit those things or find ways to help lower the stress they inflict. For example, if I'm driving somewhere new I make sure to look it up on the map well in advance of my travels to try and familiarize myself with the route, I look up where there is parking, I can go to Google and see if there's images of the location to help me, and if it's not far away I can even do a test run and drive there a few days before so I know where I'm going and it's less stressful on the day. I also make sure to leave early in case something happens, as being in a rush will just add to my stress.

The only warning I would give about this suggestion is that you don't want to avoid all your triggers so much that you never go out and do anything. Be thoughtful with what you avoid and what you try to work around. Don't let your avoidance keep you from living your life. If there's something that is easily avoidable, great! Avoid it. But if it's going to any new place, then don't stop yourself from going there or trying new things, just try to find ways to help limit the stress involved.

Weighted Blankets. If you have anxiety and stress and it's keeping you up at night, try sleeping with a weighted blanket. They make these specifically for anxiety and stress. There's apparently something about feeling that weight on you that helps you feel more grounded and safe and lowers your stress/anxiety. Try it!

15
Happiness Starts with You

If you've ever seen my TEDx Talk (you can watch it here: https://www.youtube.com/watch?v=0kysyaviIjg&t=2s, or search for "Corrina Thurston TEDx" on YouTube) you know I speak a lot about happiness and ways to increase your happiness levels. Many of those ways are remarkably simple, so simple that at first I didn't believe they would work.

One of the best ways to increase your happiness is simply to do a daily gratitude journal or gratitude meditation. All you have to do is write down or think about at least ten things for which you're grateful.

The trick?

Do it EVERY DAY.

The reason this works is because you are retraining your brain and directing its focus to the positive things in your life.

The more you practice this, the more your brain will naturally start to search out the good things in your daily life. The more you do this practice, the more you will flip your perspective on life.

For example, I went from having reactions like, "Ugh, I can't believe I broke another glass! What the hell is wrong with me?" to reactions like, "Well, at least I didn't cut myself or cause damage to anything else."

Do you see the difference?

The same event happened: I broke a glass. But I had retrained my brain to focus on the positive aspects of a situation instead of dwelling on the negative.

You can do this by thinking about or writing down the things you're grateful for every day.

- I'm grateful for my family.
- I'm grateful for my child.
- I'm grateful for my pets.
- I'm grateful for my home and a warm place to live.
- I'm grateful for my bed and warm blankets and comfy pillows.
- I'm grateful for sunny days and fresh air.
- I'm grateful for clean water to drink and good food to eat.
- I'm grateful for hot water and indoor plumbing!
- Etc. etc.

Plus you can focus on the small things **each day** (within the last 24 hours) to help you start to train your brain to search out the positive aspects of your daily life.

- I'm grateful my partner made dinner last night so I wouldn't have to.
- I'm grateful we didn't get as much snow as the forecast predicted.
- I'm grateful I remembered to order those things I need.
- I'm grateful I got out for a walk today.
- I'm grateful everyone was on time today.
- I'm grateful for the compliment that person gave me.
- I'm grateful for those five minutes I had to myself.
- And so on.

The more you start reminding yourself to look for the positive things in your life, the more you're training your brain. Eventually, your brain will start to look for the positives on its own and your outlook on life and every situation will be better.

This doesn't just mean your reaction to when something goes wrong – it can filter into every aspect of your life, including your self-image and confidence. When you're standing in the mirror you start noticing fewer of your flaws and more of your qualities. You do this because you're training your brain to focus on the good and when it's doing that, it doesn't have the ability to dwell on the "bad."

Something I think a lot of us fall into is the habit of looking for happiness in the next thing. You'll be happier when you go to college. You'll be happier when you graduate. You'll be happier when you're married. You'll be happier when you make more money and get a promotion. You'll be happier when you buy a house. You'll be happier when you have kids. You'll be happier when you lose weight. Etc.

But here's the thing: **if you're always looking for happiness in the next thing, then you're never going to feel true happiness in the present.** This means you'll never truly be happy.

If you can't stop and look at your current life and start to see the good in it, no matter how small, then nothing in the future is going to change that. If you can't focus on the NOW and enjoy a sunny day or a good meal or a funny conversation, then what makes you think you'll be able to once your job changes or you are married or you have kids or your kids have left, etc?

Absolutely no material thing or specific event is going to make you gain real happiness. It can help you feel happy for a brief moment, especially when you feel the accomplishment of achieving a goal, but then it will fade and you'll be left with how you feel on a daily basis.

Life is a series of moments, of minutes and hours and days, and if you can't find the beauty and joy in each day as it arrives, your happiness will suffer.

Again, the daily gratitudes are key.

I challenge you to keep a gratitude journal with at least ten things for which you're grateful every day for a month and see if you feel any different.

Then keep doing it.

Happiness is internal, not external. There's nothing external that can make you happy, it's all about your perspective and what drives you as a person. Even if something good happens, some people are so negative and in such a negative spiral in their minds they will see only the negativity. For example, if someone wins second place for some sort of competition, the positive person will be grateful and proud whereas the negative person will focus only on the fact that they didn't win first place.

Now, one problem is that many of the people who focus too much on the negative aspects of their lives don't realize they do it. It's a habit that has formed and even though they might be able to see it in other people, they might not recognize it in themselves.

This type of perspective will slowly wear you down, as well as the people around you. I've had to explain to multiple people about how their negativity is toxic to themselves and their loved ones, and most of them didn't realize it.

So take notice of your reactions to things. When something bad happens, even something small, do you swear and feel like a failure and think only about the bad, or do you recognize that the situation could have been a lot worse and are grateful that it's not? When something good happens, do you always wish it was better in some way, or are you grateful for the good?

I don't want to mislead you and have you think I'm happy all the time. No one is. But I used to be severely depressed and horribly negative. In the eighth grade, I won two awards at graduation and I was the only student to ever do that. I should have been thrilled, correct? Well, I was mad because there was another award I should have won and didn't. I dwelled on it for months. I deserved that other award, which is fine, but it made me not even able to recognize I should still be proud and happy with the two awards I DID win that were unexpected. When people would congratulate me on my awards, I would turn sour and mumble something about not getting the other award. It was a completely unnecessary negativity that was toxic for myself and those around me.

That's the type of thing we do without realizing it, especially if we have expectations of some kind and they aren't met.

I'm a different person now, and the reason is because I

started to retrain my brain to focus on the positive, and less on the negative. It doesn't mean I'm constantly happy, it just means I have a better perspective on life and I'm much, much happier most of the time than I ever was before.

What would you give to be even a little bit happier? Would you give the two minutes a day it takes to write down ten things for which you're grateful?

Think about your life. You'll make time for the things that are truly a priority to you. So my question is: Is your happiness a priority?

16

Tips for Before a High-Stress Event

Let's start by defining a "high-stress event." For some
people this will only occur every once in a while when they give a
presentation at work or have a difficult discussion with a loved one,
etc. For those of us who have more anxiety, however, this could
happen almost every day. Shopping might be a high-stress event.
Going to class, socializing, or driving somewhere might be a high-
stress event.

A high-stress event is anything that causes you to feel
overwhelmed and so nervous you're uncomfortable.

Now, let's get to the tips for how to help you prepare for
these moments if you know it's going to happen in advance. We
don't always know these events are going to happen, your friend or
loved one might start an argument you were completely unprepared
for, but some of them we do know in advance.

So what do you do to help lower your stress in advance of a
high-stress event? Try some of these and see if they help:

Go slow, leave extra time. Have you ever noticed when
you're in a rush, everything is more stressful? When you only have
a short amount of time to get somewhere and you're running late or
just barely on time, your anxiety can jump, you might feel guilty, and
your stress levels rise.

Why do we constantly do this to ourselves?

It's up to you when you leave for an appointment or event or social occasion. It's up to you how much time you give yourself to get there or to get ready to leave, etc.

So give yourself more time!

Say it takes you 45 minutes to get ready to go, an hour to drive to location, and five minutes to park and walk in to the building. Therefore, you might think you need to give yourself exactly one hour and 50 minutes, right?

Wrong.

What if you run into traffic?

What if your car won't start or you realize you need to get gas too?

What if you screw up your makeup getting ready and have to start over, or spill something and have to change?

What if there's construction or you can't find a parking spot?

These things happen all the time and yet we hardly ever prepare for them by adding more time, just in case.

Instead of an hour and 50 minutes, give yourself two hours and ten minutes. If you get there early, good for you! Do some of these other tips below before you go into the building so you feel even better right before the event.

Breathe. If you get there early feel free to spend a few minutes in your car to relax and focus on your breathing, which is meditation. Breathe from your belly as this is the type of breath that is proven to lower your anxiety. Close your eyes and focus on nothing but your (deep) breathing.

Walk. Step out of your car and go for a quick walk. Walking is a great way to reduce anxiety and stress. It's amazing what a walk can do for your body, as I've said before. Try to walk nonstop for fifteen minutes at a good pace and see how you feel afterwards! (But maybe don't push yourself too much right before a presentation or interview and make yourself out of breath or sweaty....)

Stretch. Similarly, you can stretch. Remember how I said before that your muscles could hold onto toxins and stress? Do a little stretching before your event to help loosen yourself up. Get the blood flowing, clear out the toxins, loosen your muscles, and make your body feel better. If you're like me and tend to shake or quiver when you're nervous, stretching can help prevent some of that. The tighter your muscles are to begin with, the more likely they'll quiver when you're nervous.

Walking and stretching also help to warm your body up. This is great if you tend to shake as well because when you're chilly, your body is tighter and more likely to shake. When you walk and stretch you're increasing blood flow and the amount of energy in your body, which warms you up and helps your muscles avoid the dreaded nervous quiver.

Power Poses. Stand like Superman. I'm serious. If you're embarrassed to do it where people might see you, go to a bathroom and simply stand tall with your hands on your hips, looking straight ahead, for at least **two minutes**. This is one of the best "power poses" that have been scientifically proven to decrease your cortisol levels (the fight or flight hormone) and increase your testosterone levels. These two things help you be calmer and increase your confidence levels, respectively.

Doesn't that sound perfect for a high-stress event?

Think about this with your body language whenever you're out and about. When you're sitting in a waiting room about to have an important job interview, instead of sitting leaning forward, hunched over your phone, lean back and open your chest. Put an arm across the back of a chair next to you if you need to help open up your chest. This not only projects confidence to those around you, it actually helps the chemistry in your body make you FEEL more confident. It's a win-win.

Lemon water or mints. Do you suffer from nausea when you're nervous or stressed? Try strong peppermints. Peppermint is great for your digestive tract and can instantly help your nausea if you suck on a strong peppermint. It HAS to be peppermint though; wintergreen or spearmint doesn't work, unfortunately. I'm not a huge fan of peppermint, but I've never found anything as helpful for nausea as strong mints! (Warning: Do NOT use peppermint essential oil for this use. Pure peppermint can burn you.)

Lemon is another ingredient that can help people with their nausea, so lemon water is great. It also helps cleanse your mouth and throat so if you're going to be speaking at all you will be less likely to get phlegm or have your mouth get dry.

Lose your expectations. The only way you can be disappointed in something is if you have expectations going into it. Lose 'em (or at least lessen them). Try to go into experiences with an open mind. If you're holding an event, try not to get too caught up on how many people show up, but on the quality of the experience instead. With fewer expectations in life, you're open to experiment and learn from your experiences rather than always evaluating them on quantitative data. You'll be happier and less focused on potential negatives (not meeting your predefined expectations). When you don't have strict expectations for something it frees you up to focus more on the positives and what the experience IS versus what you thought it might be.

Don't ever expect to be accepted or successful with something either. **Have high hopes and low expectations, that way you're especially excited if something is successful, but not as disappointed if something is not.**

Here's an example: Last year I received a rejection letter after applying to be a part of a group art exhibit. This is not unusual, except that I'd been accepted the four years prior to that same exhibit and I had even been an award winner the previous year. Because of that I assumed I would be accepted and had those expectations without realizing it and was taken aback for a moment when I opened the rejection letter. I'd won the People's Choice award at the exhibit the last year, how was I not even accepted this year?

After that initial shock and confusion, I just shrugged and tossed it on my pile of rejections and moved on to the next thing.

Even if you do get disappointed, there's no point in dwelling, my friend.

Positive Thoughts. You should do this every day, but don't forget to also praise yourself before a high stress event. Even if you're not feeling like the phrases are accurate at that moment, you need to say them. Turn that voice inside your head from a worried, negative Nancy, to a positive, raving fan.

Repeat after me:

- I am strong.
- I am important.
- I am intelligent.
- I am talented.
- I am attractive.
- I am happy.
- I am a good person.
- I am loved.
- I am worthy.
- I am capable.

Music. Do you have music that pumps you up and makes you feel better? Listen to it on your way to your high-stress event! Or during your walk.

Avoid stimulants and depressants. Trust your body and the tips above to get you through your stressful situation. You don't need sugar, caffeine, alcohol, or anything else to help you get through it and if you have those things before your event, it's more likely to make your stress worse. Instead, have some fruit and veggies that help clear your mind and feed your body. When you think about food and drinks, think this: **Am I fueling my health or fighting it?** Then make your choice.

Repeat your motto. Don't have a motto? That's okay, you can use mine: "Whatever happens, happens."

I say this to myself when I'm really nervous about something that's going to happen. I only have so much control over a situation, so it's good to remind myself that whatever is going to happen, is going to happen. It's not my responsibility to be perfect. I don't need to try to control everything.

Neither do you.

Whatever happens, happens.

17
Attempt Your Fears

Ignore the fact that this sounds cliché and bear with me as I explain.

When I say you should attempt your fears, I don't necessarily mean climbing into a tank of venomous snakes. What I mean is, try to do things that make you nervous, *even though* they make you nervous. Things that make you even just a little uncomfortable can have a huge impact on your self-confidence and your abilities moving forward.

I'm not good at driving to new places or meeting new people. Both of those are anxiety triggers for me, so the other day when my loved one asked me to drive somewhere I'd never been and give something to someone I'd never met, I hesitated. That knee-jerk reaction of "Oh, please no," kicked in instantly. Then I said I would try (it was going to be after running errands), but not to be disappointed if I didn't get to it. He said that was fine.

Even though I was a bit uncomfortable, and tired after the day I'd had, I knew this would be a load off for my loved one, so I pushed myself to drive the extra miles and knock on this person's door. Afterward, I congratulated myself and drove home.

It was a simple thing, but it involved two of my known triggers, which get worse when you're already tired. I recognized that, gave myself an out if I didn't feel up to it after my long day (to lower my loved one's expectations on me), but then pushed myself to do it, feeling better afterwards. With that one action I had done something nice for two people, plus I'd pushed myself a little outside my comfort zone.

The more you attempt to do things that are outside your comfort zone, even small things, the better you'll get at it and the larger your comfort zone will become. Stretch it. Push the boundaries of that comfort zone to continuously make it a little bigger and a little bigger.

I'm scared all the time.

All the time.

I don't mean once a week or only when I leave the house. I mean every minute of every day.

I have anxiety and that's part of how it works.

However, I no longer let it control me, and because of that, it's no longer overwhelming. I don't feel that fear as much as I used to. I don't feel like I'm being crushed. I no longer wish I could just curl into a ball and hide. I no longer want to disappear.

As I've mentioned before, there have been times when my anxiety was so bad I drove over an hour to a gallery to drop off a piece of artwork and then couldn't get myself to walk inside.

Seems ridiculous, right? But that's what anxiety can do to you and it doesn't always make sense. It can crush you without anyone on the outside realizing what's happening. And at least for me, there's always that little voice inside the back of my head saying how ridiculous it is to be so overwhelmed just trying to decide what to wear or to buy groceries or to say hi to someone, but that voice is small and trapped in the back, unable to help me do anything about it.

I've driven over an hour to a gallery to drop off a piece of artwork before... and couldn't get myself to go inside, so I sat out in the car bawling.

I've gone grocery shopping...and left empty handed, crying on my drive home for feeling foolish and overwhelmed – and still hungry.

I've missed functions…because I was curled up in a ball on my bedroom floor surrounded by piles of perfectly acceptable clothing, but I was bawling and shaking and couldn't decide what to wear.

I've gone out to dinner at a restaurant… and had no food because I couldn't decide what to eat and was overwhelmed and, you guessed it, crying.

Anxiety is so foreign to those who have never experienced it because how can a functioning adult not be able to order a meal? Or buy a few groceries? Or drop off a painting? These are simple tasks, and yet when you have severe anxiety, it doesn't matter how simple it is or how many times you've done it before, or how much you realize it's not a challenging task, you still can't do it.

When you are in panic attack mode, you've lost control of your body. It's been hijacked, and if someone has never been through that before, it's almost impossible to imagine. This can make it that much harder on the person going through the panic attack because the people around him/her/them are saying, "Just pick something!" or "Hurry up, already!" or "All you have to do is walk inside!"

So what can you do about something like that? If your brain keeps getting hijacked to the point where you have no control, then what hope is there?

Lots.

Anxiety is a tricky bugger, but I've begun to figure it out, at least for myself, and hopefully it'll help you too.

I don't have panic attacks anymore.

I do all of our grocery shopping.

I don't just drop off artwork at galleries; I give speeches and teach workshops in them.

I no longer have trouble deciding what to wear or what to order/make for dinner.

So what changed? What happened to make such a drastic transformation?

Well, everything in this book, to be honest, but a big part of it was about attempting my fears and slowly pushing and growing my comfort zone.

One key factor is to PREVENT panic attacks, because once you're in the mode, it's nearly impossible to break out of it. So if you feel it coming, act as quickly as you can with some of the techniques in this book, like breathing, stretching, going for a walk (this one helps the most for me when my anxiety is bubbling up and I get what I call "bad energy"), write, draw, listen to music, dance, sing, do power poses, repeat your motto to yourself (whatever happens, happens), think those positive affirmations (I am strong, I am confident), etc.

Now, how do you actually go about attempting your fears in a way that won't push you right over the edge into panic attack mode all the time?

You start small.

You start by trying to pick out your outfit the day before.

You start by going online in the comfort of your own home, with no time limit, to see the menu at a restaurant and choosing a back up meal so that if you get overwhelmed and can't decide, you just choose the back up meal.

You start by walking into a gallery or grocery store with no purpose, just to look around and get more comfortable with the space.

You start by giving speeches in your living room to your furniture, pretending they're an audience.

You start by visualizing yourself doing whatever it is you need or want to do.

I'm still scared all the time, that part hasn't gone away.

It just doesn't matter.

Fear isn't a bad thing. Fear doesn't mean you're not courageous or strong, in fact it can mean the opposite. It takes a lot more courage to do something when you're filled with fear, than if you weren't. So if you go out there and do something, no matter how small or seemingly insignificant, despite being afraid, then you, my friend, are amazing.

The strongest, most courageous people in the world are those with anxiety. We live everyday thinking about the absolute worst things that could happen, and yet we do it anyway. When we're driving in a car, we think about what if we crashed there, what if that car hits us, what if we go off the road over there, and yet we keep driving.

Fear is not a bad thing. It means you're alive and it means you care.

A little fear can be good for you, so take it in baby steps. Grab your keys and drive your car somewhere you've never driven before, if that makes you nervous. Walk into a place you've never been. Try to talk to someone you don't know. And work your way up to teaching that workshop or giving that speech or going for that job interview or asking for that promotion/raise or changing your career or asking that person on a date or anything else.

There are a few things to keep in mind as you do this:

1. **Start small.** If you're easily overwhelmed, which is common with anxiety, then don't jump into giving the presentation if you're having panic attacks trying to just talk to a stranger a the check-out counter. Work your way up slowly.

2. **Realize things aren't as scary as they seem.** The more you do these little things, the more comfortable you'll get doing them and you'll start to realize you didn't need to be nearly as afraid as you were leading up to it. (Then try to remember that feeling the next time you try something new!)

3. **It's revitalizing.** There's something revitalizing and transformational about doing something that makes you nervous…and succeeding. It gives you almost a high feeling, an adrenaline rush, and it is a huge source of fuel for your self-confidence.

NOTE: Risk Tolerance. Everything we're talking about in this chapter is associated with something called Risk

Tolerance. As you might guess, this is how much you can tolerate risk.

Some people are born with a higher risk tolerance than others. There are people who are the first to line up to volunteer for something, who jump out of airplanes, who drive race cars and easily stand in front of a crowd or ask for what they want.

Then there are those of us with a low risk tolerance level and are the opposite.

The good news is that you can increase your risk tolerance. It's the same thing as increasing your comfort zone and it's done in the same way where you slowly force yourself to do things for which you are slightly uncomfortable and nervous.

Your risk tolerance level IS your comfort zone. It surrounds you like a bubble and it can change from day to day and year to year. After our current 2020 pandemic quarantine, I'm sure many people's risk tolerance has decreased and their bubble has shrunk some because they got used to being at home and not having to engage as much with the outside world. Having been mostly bedridden for 6 years, I know exactly what that's like.

In other years you might start teaching a lot of workshops or trying a lot of new things or get a new job, and your risk tolerance level increases and your bubble gets bigger.

When your bubble is small, it's touching you all the time and you're always at the edge of your comfort zone, always uncomfortable and nervous.

When your bubble is bigger, it's harder to reach the edge and you can do more without that discomfort and those nerves pushing on you. You're freer and more confident.

This is a process that happens slowly, but if you keep doing it you'll suddenly stop one day in the grocery store and realize you are no longer nervous going to the check-out counter. Or you realize you got dressed that day without any issues. Or you walk up to your boss and ask them for a promotion or raise in a way you wouldn't have had the courage to do before.

It's a slow process, but the realization that it's working will hit you suddenly.

It's not that you're no longer afraid, it's how you handle and manage your reactions to that fear. It no longer possesses you. It no longer hijacks your body. It's no longer in control.

You're in control, now, and that fear can take a back seat.

18
The Depression-Anxiety
Connection

Self-doubt isn't typically something that happens by itself, usually it's accompanied, if not outright *caused* by, depression and/or anxiety.

I have struggled with both depression and anxiety for most of my life. I didn't always know that's what it was, though, I just thought I was different. I thought I didn't like people. Turns out my feeling different and out of place and "darker" than other people was my depression. And my not liking people was actually social anxiety masquerading as a personality trait.

Here's something to remember: depression and anxiety are not part of you.

Let me say that again: depression and anxiety are not actually a part of you. They are not personality traits. They don't define you; they're not integral to your state of being. They're more like leeches that have attached themselves to you and you walk around feeling like they've become a part of you because you can't get them off.

Meanwhile, they continue to suck the life out of you.

Growing up, I didn't really know what depression or anxiety was, so I thought it was part of my personality.

Especially when you start having depression so young (8 years old), it feels like you've had it forever and it's just who you are.

Once you feel real happiness and confidence, however, you can look back and see how the depression and anxiety tried to shape you and change you and make you think things that weren't true.

Humans, even us introverts, are social beings, as I've said. It's in our makeup to need socialization in order to have and maintain our emotional health. There's a saying in the addiction/recovery world that sums this up: "The opposite of addiction isn't sobriety, it's connection." That quote is by Johann Hari who gave a TED Talk on the subject.

I personally think that depression, anxiety, substance misuse disorders, violence/incarceration, suicide, self-doubt, and more are all connected. If we were all happier I think there would be less of it all. Even things like bullying. The happier you are, the less likely you'll search for more happiness in the wrong places. The less likely you'll be mean to other people, or let them be mean to you. The less likely you'll feel the need for a substance to help fill that void, take that edge off, or take the pain away. The less likely you'll feel bad about yourself.

I wish we taught happiness in schools. There are so many techniques – many of which are laid out in this book – we could teach kids in school so they go into their adult life more prepared to handle stress, grief, transitions, new things, relationships, and so many other things.

School should teach us:
- How to do our taxes
- How to buy a house
- How to save for retirement
- How to keep a checkbook and do bookkeeping
- Home maintenance
- Car maintenance

102

- Happiness and stress management techniques
- How to cook healthy meals
- How to sew
- How to do CPR and the Heimlich Maneuver
- Basic self-defense
- And more.

If we learned these things in school from a young age, do you know how much more confident we would be going into our adult lives? These are ESSENTIAL things for us to know, and yet no one teaches them to us when they have us as literally a captive audience every day as children.

Of course you're going to have self-doubt when you do your taxes for the first time or buy your first car or try to start a business or go for your first job interview or accidentally find yourself in a dangerous situation…no one taught you what to do! No one taught you how to control your fear and panic in an emergency situation. No one taught you how to negotiate for a raise. No one taught you how to prepare your taxes, what to include in a contract, etc.

"Adulting" has become everyone feeling like a child who is pretending they know what they're doing as an adult.

Now of course this isn't true for everyone, and as you get older some things get better because your comfort zone grows.

But imagine if you had learned that stuff in school. Just imagine!

Now, it's one thing when it's a task like keeping a checkbook that is easily described and taught. It's a whole other ball game when it comes to something like happiness and self-confidence, which is triggered by different things for different people, and is less of an exact practice.

However, if we could teach kids to meditate at a young age, I bet all the money in my pockets they would be able to focus better and feel calmer and handle stress much better both as children and when they become adults.

If we could teach kids to keep a gratitude journal and write

103

down 10+ things every day for which they're grateful (which takes all of 60 seconds, so it's not going to eat into their busy school day), I bet they'd have a more positive outlook on life.

If we could teach kids power poses and breathing techniques and to do positive affirmations, I bet they would feel more confident and empowered.

So why aren't these things part of the curriculum?

If there are schools out there willing to try this out, I hope they contact me. I know there are schools out there willing to put the emotional well-being of their students as a priority, and I have ideas for a curriculum ready that only takes a few minutes out of each school day.

But that's a different can of worms.

Back to what this book is about, which is **you**.

Use all or some of the techniques in this book and realize this: self-doubt can stem from any number of things. It can be a part of your depression, it can be caused by anxiety, it can come from other people putting you down, it can be from a lifetime of feeling like you're doing things wrong, it can be lack of socialization, it can be from having a small comfort zone, it can be just a feeling you have in your gut.

But it doesn't have to define you and it's not a part of you.

It's a leech.

It's stuck on your back and you're forced to carry it around as it sucks the life out of you.

However, as difficult as it is, leeches can be taken off. You just have to find the right remedy. You just have to know what to do.

Whether it's depression, anxiety, suicidal thoughts, addiction to a substance, or self-doubt, you CAN learn to manage it. You can learn to release your anger, lessen your fears, and boost your self-confidence.

You can get the leeches off.

You can feel better.

19
More on Socialization

As I write this particular chapter, it's July 2020. I don't usually like to put dates in my books because it, well, dates them, and as years go on they will feel less and less pertinent, but here's why I bring this up:

I'm sitting in my family's camp with my son and my two cats. There's a light breeze on the water of the lake out the windows and birds are flitting about the branches of the trees, capturing the interest of my cats and thankfully distracting them from each other so there's no fighting.

I bounce my 7-month-old in my lap and he's giggling and smiling, showing me his two new teeth that popped out over the last week, and everything seems normal.

Only, it's not.

We're supposed to be in Indianapolis for a wedding right now. My sister-in-law is supposed to be on a plane here tomorrow, and I should have consulting and speeches booked throughout the year.

None of those things are happening.

Instead, it's the COVID-19 global pandemic and my son is meeting everyone with face masks. Instead of starting to go to the local library for story time each week, we're home alone all day and he hasn't gotten any socialization with other kids.

Schools are trying to decide how to proceed and some are

only having kids in class two days a week, wearing masks all day, and then supposed to be homeschooled the other three days. This means parents are expected to homeschool their children more often than not, on top of their full-time jobs, and find someone to take care of their children during the day when they would usually be in school.

Thankfully we can stay somewhat connected with Internet allowing video chats and emails and social media, but it's limited and it's dangerous. Too much screen time isn't good for anyone, and the connection to the people on the other end doesn't feel as satisfying.

Some of the only people doing well right now, as business after business and nonprofit after nonprofit end up closing their doors for good, are the mask-makers. Who knew we would all suddenly own a bunch of face masks when six months ago hardly anyone owned one? That and the people who make hand sanitizer/disinfectant wipes.

Oh, and for some unknown reason people in the United States are hoarding toilet paper, causing a shortage.

The world has changed, and it's yet to be determined as I write this how it's going to play out in the long run. Will handshakes become a thing of the past? Will masks become normal? Will we ever be able to cough out in public without the people within a hundred feet of us all staring in horror?

Like I said in previous chapters, we are social animals. It's written in our DNA that we need socialization in order to maintain our emotional health. Even the introverts. The problem is, right now it is especially hard to do.

Plus, when this pandemic ends and we're allowed to gather in groups again, many of us will be out of practice and our self-doubt is going to creep in and our social anxiety is going to be stronger than ever.

I think we underestimate the importance of socialization in our lives and our emotional health. It's one of those things a lot of people took for granted and then when something like this pandemic hits, it struck hard.

I had already gone through this before. Not a pandemic, but having all my socialization suddenly taken away. When I was 18 I became very ill and then was mostly bedridden for 6+ years. Because of this, I already knew what it was like to lose that socialization, as well as many other things, all at once. I know the effect it can have. I know how a devastating a sudden strike like that to your normal way of life can be.

Now I have a son and it makes me nervous because I know how important socialization is. I know what it can do to a person to not have it.

So I'm telling you, even if you don't feel like it, you need to find ways to socialize. Make it online if you have to, in person even with social distancing if you can. You need to see people. You need to talk. You need to listen.

Connection is one of the keys to happiness and fulfillment. It makes us feel better about ourselves. It makes us feel heard and important and useful.

Go find your people, the ones that like the things you like and get excited about the things you get excited about. Go find them and talk and connect with them, in some way. Pick up the phone and call them.

It's vital that you do.

20
Speaking with Confidence

First of all, remember this: **your voice has every right to be heard.**

I don't care who is in the room. You could be in a room with a farmer, custodian, director of a nonprofit, a billionaire, a professional athlete, a teacher, a food worker, a head of state, and a famous celebrity, and no matter who you are or what you do for a living, your voice has a right to be heard, just like theirs.

That's the first and most important thing to keep in mind.

Even if you feel out of place or less than those around you for some reason (you're not), you have a right to speak. That, of course doesn't guarantee those people will listen, as we've become a society more challenged with our ability to listen to others, but you have a right to speak and if you speak with confidence, it'll help you be heard.

There are so many of us who are capable and accomplished and even in roles of authority who undermine ourselves with negative self-talk and who constantly belittle ourselves both in private and in public. I've been in meeting after meeting where there is a highly intelligent, accomplished, talented, capable person who has lessened the impact of their message by going on and on about some minor flaw they had. Whether it was their inability to prepare as much as they'd hoped, or they didn't feel like they're good public speakers so they kept apologizing (when really the only problem with the speech was them apologizing over and over), or the way they looked, etc., it was a distraction and unnecessary.

Don't sabotage yourself and your message by calling attention to your flaws or apologizing profusely for anything. If you aren't as prepared as you'd hoped, apologize once, briefly, and move on.

Most of our flaws are not nearly as bad as we think they are, and us calling attention to them and bringing them up over and over again does us no good. More than that, it doesn't do anyone else any good either. Your audience doesn't want to hear you fretting and apologizing and worrying, they want to hear what you actually have to say.

So say it.

Imposter Syndrome is real. That's why there's a whole chapter about it in this book, but it's important to remember you can show confidence even when you're not feeling it, and it will help. Remember, confidence is one of the only things I highly recommend faking. The more you go out there and fake your confidence, the more you'll start to feel it become real.

We sabotage ourselves far too often and it makes people doubt us, because it is so obvious that we doubt ourselves.

Speaking with confidence will help you be better respected, get better employment, have better conversations, gain more self-esteem, make better connections, have more authority, and realize more of your potential.

So…how do you speak with confidence, even if you're not feeling it, you wonder?

Let's get into it:

Stop hesitating. Hesitation has a useful purpose, to be sure, but the more you hesitate when you are talking about something, the less confident you'll come across to those around you. Ask yourself, why are you hesitating? Is it because you're actually not sure what you're saying is correct? Or are you just nervous?

There's a difference between hesitating and filtering before you speak. A filter can be a good thing. Hesitation is typically a sign of not having enough confidence in yourself or what you're saying.

Filters are good because they help you plan what you're going to say accordingly instead of saying anything that pops into your head. I've been a part of groups where I didn't say much, but when I did say something it always had purpose. It had conviction. It had depth and importance to the conversation at hand. So even though I didn't speak nearly as often as some of the people in the group, when I did it was clear that what I said had value and people were listening.

Hesitation is different. Hesitation, which I've also struggled with in groups many times, makes it much easier for another person to interrupt and walk all over you. It gives your words less impact and people won't be listening as intently. It makes you seem less like an authority and more like someone out of place, even if you're not. It can make people question, even just slightly, your knowledge and abilities.

But you can fix it!

You can catch yourself doing it in a conversation and change it. You can go into a meeting thinking about it beforehand and try to prepare yourself to speak clearly and with purpose.

Hesitation is one of those things you build into yourself as such an ingrained habit that it will take practice and time before you really see a difference and get the hang of it. That's okay. Even a *little* less hesitation will help you seem more confident and reinforce what you're saying.

Sometimes you even hesitate when someone asks about you, which is silly because who knows you better than you? Nobody. Of all the subjects, that's the one where you should have the most confidence! Don't let your discomfort talking about yourself (hello, self-doubt!) make you hesitate when you're asked a question. Treat it like any other subject. If someone asks a question about what you do or what you like, pretend as if you're speaking about someone or something else. Take the self-doubt out of it by treating it like it's not about you, it's about a subject you know lots about.

Use assertive, commanding phrases. What I mean by this

is, if someone asks you to do something, instead of saying something like, "I think that might be okay," say: "I can do that."

Can you hear the difference?

Words like, "might," "possibly," "could," "suppose," and others are passive and you don't sound as confident when you use them. They are much weaker than if you use words and phrases that are crisp, clear, and concise. "Yes." "I'd like you to _____." "Tell me more about _____." "I can do that."

This doesn't mean you should say you can do something you can't or make people believe you're more capable at something than you really are, but "I can try," is a lot more confident and triggers more respect than saying, "I'm not sure. I've never done anything quite like it before. I suppose I could maybe try to do that…"

Speak in positives. On a similar note, it's stronger to say "that's good," than to say it in the negative form, "that's not bad."

Those of us with self-esteem issues tend to use the negative version of many phrases, whether it's self-talk or the way we phrase something to others. It's a habit you get into, but it weakens your words.

Be aware of your posture. As we've talked about in previous chapters, posture can be a huge part of overcoming self-doubt and showing confidence, even if you're not fully feeling that way. Straighten your back, pull your shoulders back, and lift your head UP. Look more confident, act more confident, and you'll begin to feel more confident.

Be engaged. People are going to take you more seriously and see you as more confident if you are NOT stuck to your phone and if you're an active, engaged listener back to them. You can't expect someone to listen to you if you don't take the time and energy to listen to them. So put the phone away. Keep your head up, make eye contact, and nod and respond when appropriate.

If you can connect with whomever it is you're talking with on a level deeper than chit-chat, it'll help in all ways, including your confidence levels. Listen to what they're saying. Connect some part of your life and knowledge to what they're talking about to show that you understand and have that connection.

If you're talking to someone with whom you don't feel much connection, that's okay. It happens. You know what? You might even be awkward. But you know what else? It's not a big deal.

I'm awkward all the time. Really, just ask anyone who has ever met me. I finished a conversation the other day with the manager of a venue and my partner was with me and as soon as we walked out of the building and out of earshot he bent over laughing and said, "You're SO AWKWARD!"

I was like, "It wasn't THAT bad."

"Yes it was! You were so awkward!"

"Hey, people LIKE my awkwardness, mkay? And he was awkward too!"

"That's true, I'm not saying it was a bad thing, I love your awkwardness, but it was real!"

Ahem.

Despite being awkward apparently to the point of my partner laughing so hard he had to stop walking… I'm writing books and giving speeches and teaching workshops and I'm a mom and an entrepreneur and wife and friend. I can still be all those things and be awkward sometimes (a lot of the time?). I can still be those things despite my fears and self-doubt and guilt and illnesses.

Don't ever feel like you can't be you, awkwardness and all. Take it in stride. You'll still connect with people. Just try to be the more confident version of you, that person you WANT to be in public, that person you visualize yourself being. It can happen, with practice.

Say, "I don't know." I had my 5-year-old niece over for dinner the other night and something came up in conversation she didn't understand, so she said she didn't know what we meant. Before I explained what we were talking about, I took a moment to congratulate and thank her for admitting she didn't know, because it's not an easy thing to do.

You can say, "I don't know," and still sound confident.

Just say it. Without hesitation or fear of being judged, you can say you don't know something and because you say it clearly and with confidence, people won't think much of it.

When I say I don't know something, I look expectantly at those around me waiting for them to explain. When you say it hesitantly you're putting yourself in the spotlight for not knowing something. When you say it with confidence and look at those around you expectantly, the spotlight goes straight back to them.

Power Poses. As I've written before, don't forget to throw some power poses in there as well, either before you are talking with whomever to boost your confidence beforehand, or just stand or sit with your back straight and chest open. If you have trouble doing that, having a hand on your hip can help put your back into that position without seeming too awkward or uncomfortable. Many times I'll be talking to someone with one hand on my hip to help my body stay in at least a partial power pose and help my confidence. It also makes you SEEM more confident, even if you're not. There's a reason so many leaders go to this position naturally when they're talking.

Speaking with confidence is hard when you suffer from self-doubt or issues with self-esteem. Your inclination is to be quiet, that your voice isn't as important as those around you, to curl into yourself and look down.

Essentially, you're hiding. As much as you can in a public situation, you're hiding and hoping no one notices you.

Whether it's because of a lack of self-confidence, or social anxiety, or depression, or feeling out of place, your instinct might be to hide away.

I get it. That's me too. In a networking event, I was typically the one in the corner focused intently on the cup of tea in my hand, hoping the only people who noticed me would be people I already knew, which is obviously not the point of a networking event. It didn't matter, though, because my self-doubt and anxiety were in control and I didn't feel like I had anything worth saying. I didn't feel like I belonged in the room. I felt awkward and vulnerable and exposed. I felt like at any moment people were going to think I was some kind of fraud or judge me or just straight up find me boring.

I still have this instinct to hide away, especially in big groups of people I don't know. The trick is to learn to ignore it. Push that instinct aside and stand up straight with your head up, making eye contact with those that pass by, saying hi and engaging with the crowd.

It's not someone else's responsibility to listen to you, it's your responsibility to stand up and make yourself heard. You need to make it worth their time and energy as well as make them feel like you actually want to be there.

When you're hovering in the corner, avoiding eye contact and fiddling with your phone or drink, your body language is giving out all sorts of "No" signals.

If you want to make progress, if you want to be respected and heard and add value to a situation, then you have to make an effort to be inviting. Relax your neck and shoulders and brow and jaw. Stop holding so much tension in between your shoulder blades and take a deep breath. Then another. Look up and give even just a slight smile when someone looks in your direction. Put your hand on your hip to open up your body language and take a step out from the corner.

I know you feel exposed. Being in a corner is a very natural response to fear because it limits the number of sides you need to keep track of in order to stay safe. It's a primal fight or flight response to want something solid behind you so you feel safer.

Let your straight, confident posture take over that aspect. **Your back is the wall.** This is not a fight or flight situation, despite your mind trying to make it feel that way. Showing just a little bit of confidence can make you go from being the shy, timid, awkward, unengaged person in the corner no one is approaching because you're giving out all sorts of "No" vibes, to actually making useful connections, meeting interesting people, learning something new, and creating opportunities.

So much can come from speaking with confidence, not

hesitating, and using your posture/expressions to convey a relaxed and assured attitude. You got this. Your voice has every right to be heard.

Now go speak.

21
Be Vulnerable

You're not alone.

No matter what you're going through, you are not the only one going through it, even if it feels that way. You're not the only one with self-esteem issues. You're not the only one who has been a victim of trauma. You are not the only one who is chronically ill. You are not the only one in a terrible relationship. You are not the only one who regrets their life decisions. You're not the only one with suicidal thoughts. You're not the only one getting bullied or harassed. You're not the only one with an addiction. You're not the only one confused and scared.

If we were all more open about the daily struggles we face, perhaps we would realize it's a majority of people who suffer from some kind of anxiety, depression, and self-doubt. It's a majority of us who at least have moments where we feel like we're not enough. It's a majority of us who question, second-guess, and hold ourselves back from doing something we want to do because of our self-doubt.

So many things, like anxiety, depression, addiction, trauma, miscarriage, eating disorders, and others, are much more common than we realize. Why? Because we don't talk about it as much as we should.

When I got pregnant my partner and I decided we were going to tell people right away instead of waiting the typical 14 weeks that are the first trimester. Most people wait because it's in those first 14 weeks that you're most likely to have a miscarriage or something go wrong with the pregnancy. That's fine, but I knew if I had a miscarriage, I'd be telling my family and friends about that too because I didn't want to go through that alone, so I figured I might as well tell people about the pregnancy right up front and they could come along the journey with me, for better or worse.

Miscarriages are extremely common. They're much more common than we realize, and it's because we don't talk about it.

Anxiety is much more common than we realize, plaguing a huge number of people, but we don't realize it because we don't talk about it.

ALL of these things – addiction, trauma, illness, chronic pain, depression, suicidal thoughts, self-doubt, Bi-polar and other disorders – are incredibly common and not talked about nearly enough.

There's stigma attached to having some sort of mental health issue, even if it's temporary. But when you know how common it is to have a mental health issue, that stigma becomes ridiculous.

One of the reasons people connect with me or listen to me or follow my lead is because I talk openly about *all the things* and it makes them feel better about themselves and like it's okay to feel how they're feeling.

Because it is.

Your feelings and emotions and struggles are valid. They are legitimate.

There are things like anxiety and depression that you can't fully understand unless you've been there. It's just too hard to comprehend that a fully functioning adult could lose their mind in a grocery store and cry and shake and sweat and leave the building without getting any (needed!) food because of anxiety about something as common – and really not scary – as a check-out counter.

It doesn't make any sense.

Yet it happens. Anxiety hijacks your brain and body and if you're not prepared (and even sometimes when you are), it can make you do things that just don't make sense and you feel like you've lost control.

There's nothing worse than feeling like you don't have control over your own body/mind.

There's nothing wrong with you if you've suffered from any of these, or other, problems. You're normal, even if it doesn't feel that way.

So I'm sending out a request to anyone and everyone who reads this book: **please start being more open and vulnerable.**

Please! I'm begging you.

It's not just for you, although it will help to lighten your load and make you feel better and more confident too. It's also for all those people still too scared to admit they have a problem and too weighed down by the stigma to talk to anyone about it, feeling trapped and alone.

The more of us who talk openly about these issues, the more people who will come out of the woodwork and say, yeah, me too. The more we talk about it, the more we can normalize it and when that happens, it's much easier to help it.

This doesn't mean you need to go on and on about it or keep pointing out your flaws to your peers, as we've talked about before, but do be open and honest when something comes up in conversation.

I've had suicidal thoughts. I've been so depressed I wanted to die.

I've had severe anxiety attacks that made me unable to function at all.

I've lost opportunities due to my own self-doubt.

I've dealt with abusive people in my life.

I've suffered different types of trauma, chronic illness, and chronic pain.

I've felt like a waste of space, a waste of the air I was breathing, a waste of everyone's time and energy. A burden. A fraud. A failure.

I've felt completely worthless and raw and shattered and miserable.

I am by no means alone.

There are people out there who are even worse off than I was, which is saying something. There are millions of people right now going through things I can't even imagine, and there are millions going through very similar things to what I've been through.

It's common and normal and valid.

Unfortunately, it's far too common nowadays to feel the weight of depression and self-doubt and all the other things we've talked about. Our society is crushing us with these expectations and disconnection and misdirected anger.

We need to change the way we all discuss and deal with these issues. If we're all suffering, we can all reach out and help one another. But we can't do that if we don't even know there's a problem.

Being open and vulnerable and exposing your own issues to the world will help free the world from some of these restraints of stigma and judgment and fear. It will help you feel more whole because you'll no longer be hiding part of yourself from the world.

I was contacted by an artist a few years ago who was touched by my story after she read about me in the newspaper. She too was chronically ill and had limitations on her energy and abilities, but so far she had refused to tell anyone she was sick. Here she was thanking me for speaking out and making her feel a little better knowing that she was not the only one in this predicament, and yet she still refused to tell even her closest friends she was chronically ill.

When you purposefully hide away such a huge part of your life from the people around you, it's exhausting.

It can also cause a lot of self-doubt and guilt and misery.

If you can't explain why you can't make it to go see a friend, you may end up losing that friendship over time.

If you are constantly covering your pain with a fake smile, people aren't going to understand why you suddenly break down or keep canceling on them or don't do more regularly.

It takes a lot of effort to hide away your issues, even though it's a natural response. The question is: do you really need to hide them away?

What's making you feel like you need to cover your struggles? What's making you feel like you need to pretend you're okay when you're not?

The more you can own your struggles and limitations, the less control they have over you.

Once I realized this, a whole new world opened up. I realized instead of constantly pushing against my limitations and getting frustrated, I was going to have to find ways to work with and around them. I needed to change my perspective and how I dealt with these issues in my daily life. I needed to be proactive. I needed to own up to what was happening to me and explain it to those around me so they could understand it better, and maybe I could too.

I met with a friend the other day. I hadn't seen her in two years and we don't talk that much, but we've been friends since grade school. She told me that she needed advice and she came to me because of two things: 1.) She felt like I wasn't going to judge her for how she felt about something and she could be honest and voice her fears about why she was hesitating about this particular thing. 2.) She knew I wouldn't bullshit her. She knew I would give her answers that were honest and blunt and tell it the way it is.

Initially I cultivated this reputation by accident. It wasn't until I'd been more open for a while that I realized the effect it was having on both myself and those around me.

I get emails all the time from people thanking me for being so open, raw, and honest. It's not something I initially thought would happen. I was shocked at the first few times people came up to me and showed so much gratitude just for telling my story in public.

Gratitude for being open.

Gratitude for being vulnerable.

You are not alone. Stop making yourself feel like you're alone by keeping everything to yourself and hiding away your struggles, feeling guilty, and pushing people away. You don't have to hide the "bad" parts of yourself. You are who you are and you are NOT your depression. You are NOT your anxiety. You are NOT your addiction or trauma or fears or tragedies or self-doubt.

Those things are not your personality, they're just leeches attached to you.

You are NOT defined by your struggles; you are defined by how you handle yourself and how you are as a person underneath all that baggage. Take away all those things and who are you really?

Now is a good time to self-assess. Maybe take out a piece of paper and answer these questions:

After taking away your depression, self-doubt, anger, frustration, addictions, dependencies, toxic relationships, traumas, fears, and struggles... what's left? Who are you without those things?

What would you be like, feel like, if you didn't have to deal with those things?

What do you like to do? What is an activity that you get so caught up in that you lose track of time?

What are you really good at?

Who are your favorite people to be around?

What are your favorite things about yourself?

How can you spend more time doing the things you love, with the people you love, and accentuate the things you love most about yourself?

Stop thinking of yourself as a collection of your issues. You are not depression; you are a person suffering from depression. You can overcome it and it can go away and you are still going to be you.

You are not an addict; you are a person suffering from an addiction.

Do you hear the difference?

I know it doesn't always feel that way. Self-doubt and anxiety and depression can be so overwhelming and do such a good job hijacking your brain and body it can feel as though you are nothing without them. You feel like you are depressed, and that's it.

That's what/who you are.

It's not.

I was depressed at such a young age and for so long I thought I was just a "dark" person. Turns out I'm not.

My social anxiety started so young and was so overwhelming I thought I just didn't like people. Turns out that was wrong too.

I am more than the collection of my symptoms and struggles.

If I am a salad (yes, I just called myself a salad, bear with me here…) those are the dressings. Sure, they can overwhelm the taste of the salad and if you have so much dressing, that's all you're going to taste. The salad is then just a crunchy delivery system for the dressing. But you can also throw that salad into a colander and rinse that dressing off. Underneath it is still the same salad. Despite how sticky and gooey and flavorful that dressing can be, it can still be washed off. You can't, however, wash the green off of a piece of kale. It will always be green.

That's the difference. Right now you might be thinking of your self-doubt like the green – something that's attached to you and inherently YOU. You might be thinking of it as a personality trait, when it isn't.

Your self-doubt is simply a reaction your body has had to the stress in your life. It can build up over time and seem like it's a part of you, but it's just dressing.

Sure, it's sticky dressing that's going to take some serious water pressure and scrubbing to get it off and find that kale underneath, but you can do it. And what you'll find beneath will be your true color and taste, who you are without your self-doubt getting in the way.

22
War of the Energies

More and more I feel like there's all kinds of energies in this world, many of which we don't know much about. We've talked a little about energy vampires before, which is a person who, not necessarily on purpose, tends to suck the energy out of those around them. This type of person can be toxic if you spend too much time with them because they just take and take and take.

How do they do that? How is it possible just being around a particular person can make you feel so drained and like your energy is gone?

Energies are weird.

There are a lot of people who form an almost tangible cloud of negative energy around them and it affects everyone with whom they come in contact. Their negative energy, despite being their own problem, filters into the energy of those around them, corrupting it and turning it negative too. Again, these people might not be doing this on purpose, but they can be toxic if you spend too much time around them.

The more I can recognize the different energies around me and inside myself, the more I feel I can use them and not let them use me. I try to shelter myself from the negative energies when I can, and soak up the positive ones. Walking, especially outside and near or in nature, is especially full of good energies for me. Being in a place without much natural light, on the other hand, tends to cause negative energy for me.

Why am I bringing this up in a book about self-doubt? Because self-doubt is a type of energy too.

We have all kinds of internal energies, and we don't always have control over them. Sometimes you're going to wake up in a bad mood. It happens. You can help by doing all the exercises and using the techniques we've talked about in this book, but it doesn't mean you had control over how you felt when you got up. On the other hand, you might be talking to someone and suddenly feel very energized and excitable. Where did that sudden energy come from?

Energies are weird. And amazing. And scary. And powerful. And important.

My sister is pretty awesome. Starting when I was sick and in college, and then sick at home (she lived across the country at the time), she started sending me cards in the mail. They're always full of words of encouragement and things for which she is grateful when it comes to me. Each one over the years lifts me up. She is essentially taking some of her good energy and using her pen to capture that energy on paper in these cute greeting cards, and then wraps them in an envelope and sends them straight to me. That energy is then filtered into me when I read what she wrote and feel the love and thoughtfulness and gratitude that went into writing it.

It's fascinating and powerful.

Giving someone a simple compliment can boost their positive energy for the rest of the day. It can also boost yours as science shows that doing something nice for someone else is one of the best ways to increase your own happiness.

I find energy is very different than something like sustenance. If you're in need of sustenance, you need to eat and it will give you the energy to move and function and last a certain amount of time before you need to eat again and get more energy.

Positive internal energies – and negative ones – are different in that the more that's put out, the more that will be created.

Energies are like breast milk (yup, breast milk), in that the more that is used, the more that is then created! With breast milk you don't create a certain amount, your body will try to create however much is needed. So if you pump AND breastfeed your child, your body is going to create more than your child actually needs and you can create a freezer stash of pumped milk for when you need to give them a bottle.

The more you use, the more you create.

Positive energies – and negative, unfortunately – are just like that! You don't have just a specific amount, the more you can use and filter into your life, the more you can create internally as well.

Here's an example:

There are two people in a room. One person has had a terrible day and lots of bad things have piled on during the day after not sleeping well and they are full of negative energies. Their mind is swirling with negative thoughts about themselves, their life, their work, and everything else. Their inner monologue is silently bashing them with phrases like "you're not good enough," "everything is going wrong," and "you're a failure." Those negative energies are playing off each other and building up more and more until that person feels like they're drowning.

The other person in the room has had a good day. They slept well and feel energized. They had some good things happen during their day, plus some friends reached out to tell them they were thinking of them. They socialized with a loved one and laughed out loud. They received hugs and humor and happiness. They are thinking about all the things for which they are grateful and are content.

Those two people – friends or family or partners – meet in a room.

Now we have the war of the energies.

In the one corner we have the negative energies, and in the other corner we have the positive energies.

The question is: which one is strong enough to overpower the other?

The two people start to have a conversation. One is focusing on the negatives, sighing and disgruntled. The other is content and happy with their day, but upon hearing the negative news and feeling that negative energy from the other person, they start to falter.

Have you ever had this happen? You're in a fairly good mood, or even a great mood, and then someone comes in with negative energy and your good vibes get squashed.

I talked about this in the chapter about "being a screen door," where you can try to empathize with your loved one, but you don't have to suck up all their negative energy like a sponge. You can still feel good inside even when they are being negative by letting it flow through you, like a breeze through a screen door.

The problem is that the negative energies can be so sudden and so overwhelming, it can be hard to remember to do this and to fight back with our positive energies.

So, let's get back to the room and start again.

The person with the negative energy walks in and starts showing their frustration with their day. Instead of letting the negative energy overwhelm and squash their own positive energy, the other person knows how to navigate the situation. Every time the negative person says something, the other person brings the conversation back to something positive. They let the person know they understand their anger and frustration, but then are able to weave the conversation back to the positive things about their own day, or they ask the person if anything good happened during their day, or they offer to take their mind off the negative stuff with a positive distraction, like a movie, a back rub, dinner out, a game of cards, going for a walk, going to a lake, snuggling, or some other activity they like to do together.

The people involved determine which side wins the war of the energies. Sometimes, negativity will win and everyone feels worse. Sometimes, positivity wins and everyone ends up feeling better, including the person who was already feeling positive. Why? Because the act of making another person feel better will also make you feel better.

Next time you're in this situation, think about it. If you're the positive one, let the negative person vent and acknowledge their struggles without soaking them up yourself, and then try to use your positive energy to help them feel better. If you're on the negative side of the spectrum and there's someone around you who is obviously feeling more positive, try not to vomit your negativity all over them, · and also try to see if there's a way you can soak up some of their positivity. Don't be jealous or resentful of their happiness, just get closer to them and try to swim in it a little bit. Ask them to help brighten your spirits with some of the things mentioned above. Tell them what's wrong, so they don't misunderstand and think they did something wrong if they didn't, and then actively try to do the things you know could help you feel better.

Unfortunately, the war of the energies is not only between two people, it's an internal struggle we go through every moment of every day. You are constantly full of positive and negative energies at once, and it doesn't take much for one to snuff out the other moment to moment.

So which one will win?

Don't worry if negativity wins sometimes. It happens. You can't always be happy and cheerful, or even mildly content. Sometimes bad things happen and you're going to be upset.

But here's the deal: when terrible things happen, you can cry. You can yell. You can bang your fist against a counter (not too hard, don't break anything or hurt yourself or scare your pets/kids/ spouse…). You can lie down and wallow in your misery, but don't let it happen for long. Limit yourself. Cry, yell into a pillow, curl up in a ball, but before long you need to go wash your face off and figure out what's next. You need to stretch and breathe and go for a walk and do a power pose and write down the things for which you're grateful and say positive things about yourself and do all the things you know could help you feel better, and move on.

Sometimes it's best to let negativity win a battle, but then you have to pick yourself up and focus on what you need to do to make sure that positivity wins the war.

Every day you have a choice. Are you going to do the simple

things – write down 10 things for which you're grateful, strike a power pose for 2 minutes while reciting positive "I am" statements in your head, focusing on your breathing for 2 minutes, etc. – to give yourself a better chance at feeling better and more confident? Are you going to prioritize your mental health and do what you can to stay positive and crush your self-doubt? Or are you going to allow that negativity that surrounds us all, especially these days, to sink and drown you?

Some people are more prone to negative thoughts than others. I am one of those people. Therefore, we have to work harder to overcome our body's tendency to dwell on the negative. We have to focus on actually doing these things regularly to keep fighting every day for our positive energy.

It's not impossible. It's also not easy. It takes dedication and a willingness to learn things about yourself you might usually try to cover up, even from yourself.

You are strong. You are capable. You are worthy.

There's a war going on in each of us every moment of every day.

Which side are you on? Which one will win today?

23
Sometimes You Need Help

It's okay if you can't power pose your way to complete happiness. Unfortunately, some of us have hormone imbalances playing a role or a genetic disposition to depression and self-doubt or other underlying factors that are made better by the techniques laid out in this book, but might not be enough.

It's okay to need more than meditation to get you through. Do the meditation, do the power poses, and do the daily gratitudes because that is going to help you no matter what, but for some individuals, you're going to need more help.

It's up to you to figure out what that is.

You might need to take a calming supplement like l-theanine, magnesium, lemon balm, lavender, or GABA.

Maybe you should be on an antidepressant.

Perhaps you'd do well talking to a therapist.

Whatever form of help works best for you is absolutely fine. I personally can't take antidepressants or anti-anxiety meds because they have the opposite reaction in my body and they make me suicidal. They tried many different types of these meds when I was around 19 years old and had just gotten sick but was yet to have an actual diagnosis.

None of it worked. In fact, I became much worse because of those meds, but that's just me. For some people those meds are a savior! So if it's something your doctor thinks you should try, don't avoid them just because of those like me who can't tolerate them. Be open to trying anything that might help, and be prepared if it doesn't.

Also remember that you need to be taking those types of meds very regularly (don't skip a dose) and they usually take 10+ days to start working in your system, so give them a little time before you give up.

This book, and future books, and my website www.findyourhappiness.info, and many of my articles only exist because I couldn't tolerate those meds.

What do you do when you are so depressed you are suicidal, but you can't take an antidepressant?

What do you do when you are so anxious you can't stop shaking and you're having panic attacks just getting tea in your own kitchen, but can't take an anti-anxiety med?

You do whatever you can to figure out other ways to help yourself.

And that's exactly what I did.

I searched and I experimented and I learned as much as I could about happiness and managing anxiety and boosting self-confidence and learning to live with limitations. I read and I watched videos and I wrote and I failed and I learned more and got up again.

I'm going to be honest, at first I was skeptical. Gratitude is the key to happiness? I was bedridden and in excruciating pain. Almost everything in my life had been ripped away from me. I was depressed, I felt like a huge burden on those around me, and I couldn't function.

What the hell did I have for which to be grateful?

I scoffed and it honestly made me a little angry (I had a lot of anger in those days) that someone thought a little gratitude would make me feel better, given my situation. It made me think that person had never been through extraordinarily difficult times and of course THEY had things for which they were grateful, their life was better than mine! Most lives were at the time.

But I kept coming back to it.

And back to it.

And back to it.

Gratitude, eh? Gratitude…

While lying in bed, after counting the dots on my ceiling for the 437th time since there's not much else to do when you're bedridden but are physically incapable of watching TV or reading… I thought, well, I suppose I was grateful I had a bed to lie on. I suppose I was grateful for the blankets to keep me warm, especially since one of my symptoms was always being cold. I guess I was grateful for my cats coming to visit me, allowing a distraction from the never-ending onslaught of terrible thoughts in my head. I was certainly grateful for my parents taking care of me, otherwise I would have starved to death very quickly, incapable of getting food or having a place to live, plus they were my only company. I was grateful for heat, a home, hot water, although taking a shower was about once a week and was an all-day chore that drained the life out of me.

As I sat in bed eating the dinner my mom had brought down to my dark little room that night, I was looking at the food differently. Where before I would just eat whatever was placed in front of me without thinking about it, that night I thought about how grateful I was I had someone to cook me meals and bring them down to me. I was grateful the food was healthy and flavorful. I was grateful for my mom's company, even though we had to whisper sometimes to talk because my migraine was so bad.

My life was terrible and I wouldn't wish it on my worst enemy, but I still had plenty of things for which to be grateful.

I just had to LOOK.

That's the trick, you see. You have to LOOK to see the good things in your life. You have to LOOK to find those many things for which you should be grateful. You have to LOOK and see all those things that others have done to help you, the opportunities you've been given, and beautiful, wonderful things that surround you.

If you don't try the meditation and the power poses and the gratitudes and the positive statements and all the other techniques, you're not giving yourself a fair shot at being happy and confident.

It's like trying to lose weight and doing some exercise but still eating lots of fatty, salty, sugary, processed foods. You might still lose a little weight, but you're not giving yourself a good base to work on. You're not giving yourself the fuel your body really needs.

So try the techniques for a month and see what happens. If they help but you don't think they're enough, it's okay to get help too. Find a therapist or try a supplement.

Your happiness and self-confidence are too important. Prioritize them. Don't shy away from what it takes because you think it's going to be too hard. Give yourself the foundation you need to build yourself up again and be the person you want to be. And remember that you can't build a foundation in a day. It takes practice and patience to keep doing these things and keep giving yourself a daily boost.

You are worthy of being a confident, happy, relaxed, self-assured, and independent person. But those are all things you have to get for yourself, you can't have someone do it for you. I can't do it for you. I can give you the knowledge and techniques that have helped many others, and me but it's up to you to actually put them into place and crush your self-doubt. It's up to you to train your brain to think about both the world and yourself in a different, more positive way.

You can do it and I'm always here to help if you need it. This isn't a subject where I want to keep any knowledge to myself; I want to get it out there for as many people as I can.

This world needs to be a happier place. We need ALL of us to be happier people and self-doubt is a big obstacle to that.

If we were all happier, a little more confident, what would the world be like?

I want to find out.

24

Imposter Syndrome

Self-doubt with a fancy name, Imposter Syndrome is something a lot of people silently struggle with, leaders and those in positions of power absolutely included.

What is Imposter Syndrome?

Imposter Syndrome goes like this: You win an award. That's all fine and dandy, but then as you look at the other candidates you surpassed to win said award, you start to feel guilty. You wonder, how did I win this award over all these other people? Why would they choose ME? You feel like at any moment someone is going to realize there was a mistake and you really aren't as qualified, or talented, and you feel like a fraud.

It's not just with awards, though, it can happen with lots of different situations. Maybe it's getting a promotion. It could be that you've been invited to be a part of some sort of group. It could be that discomfort you feel calling yourself an "artist" or an "entrepreneur" or "writer" or anything else when someone asks. It can strike at any time and at first, you might not realize it's happening.

If you're prone to nerves and social anxiety and self-doubt, it might be hard to distinguish one from the other. However, if you feel alone and out of place within a group of people, if you feel like you're not as talented or important as those around you, if you are questioning your qualifications for something, I bet Imposter

Syndrome might have its hooks in you.

It's not just nerves. Nerves alone don't make you feel unqualified. Nerves alone don't make you feel unworthy. It's more than that. It's a deep sense of guilt and fear and shame.

The problem is you can't start to fix something if you don't realize it's there. So when you're feeling uncomfortable about something, when you're feeling unqualified despite others saying you're not, stop and assess: Is this Imposter Syndrome? Why am I feeling this way?

A few years ago I was selected to be part of a group of 25 influential thought-leaders in my state. We met every couple months and discussed some of the issues in our state and the world.

I felt completely out of place.

Looking around the room, I was the youngest there. I was also the only one without a college degree, the only artist, the only entrepreneur, the only one who had ever had to suffer with a chronic illness, the only one who hadn't had the opportunity in life to travel much, and the list goes on...

What the hell was I doing there? How did they choose me out of so many other people to be a part of this group? What did I have to offer?

The first couple times we met, I kept my mouth shut. I was actively listening and enjoyed the conversations, but I had little to add. I would leave those meetings feeling both energized by the conversations, and feeling disappointed, guilty, and a bit ashamed. If I wasn't contributing like some of the others, was I just a waste of space in that room?

During our third meeting we were talking about leadership and I had also just been to a leadership conference where the guest speaker talked about "leading from within." I found this intriguing. I had always shied away from calling myself a leader because I thought it implied you actively wanted followers and it certainly comes with a responsibility to those followers. That responsibility is based on your own knowledge and I never felt like I had enough of that to state outright that I was a leader. And yet, I would naturally fall into that role again and again, willingly or not, throughout my life. I always ended up being the captain of my sports teams, the leader in a group project, the person chosen to speak at an event, etc. I distinctly remember my basketball coach calling me the "reluctant leader" of our team and my teacher in high school saying I was the "silent leader" of our class.

This speaker, however, talked about "leading from within," and what he meant was that sometimes the best leaders aren't far out ahead of the pack, they're right there with them, going through the same things at the same time, but just a little bit ahead and willing to speak up and help others if they can.

Wait a second. You can be a leader and still be going through those things yourself too?

Yes.

So when I was at my third meeting with this group of young thought-leaders, halfway through I had an epiphany and my Imposter Syndrome started to melt away.

For the first two meetings I had wondered why I was even there. My perspective was so vastly different than those around me, my experiences so unusual when compared to the other group members, that I felt I didn't fit in.

Then I realized that was exactly WHY I was there.

It was because I was different that I could speak to different issues that these other people wouldn't have even thought about because it had never affected them. It was my different experiences and perspective that made it so my voice could speak out for those similar to me and not let artists and entrepreneurs and those with chronic illnesses and those who have suffered from depression and anxiety and many other things get cut out of the conversation.

If you're in a leadership group talking about the issues in your state, you WANT different lifestyles and perspectives to be present for the conversation, otherwise you're not seeing the whole picture.

Suddenly I didn't feel quite so out of place. Instead I felt a responsibility to the people similar to me, my people, who were otherwise not represented in that room.

So I spoke up.

You know what happened?

Well, the person who was moderating the conversation at the time scrunched up their face in a "who are you to talk?" kind of way, and then didn't even write down what I'd said and moved on to the next person.

Ouch.

Talk about a body blow. Here I finally got up the courage to speak and I immediately got shut down, in front of everyone. That person tried to discredit what I said by ignoring it. Not only that, everyone else in the room let them do it without saying anything.

I'm not going to lie, that kind of pissed me off and I've found that sometimes a bit of anger can be useful in helping you overcome your self-doubt too...

"Excuse me," I said, gathering up my courage again and pulling it over me like a cloak.

Deep breath

"I have just as much right to be heard here as everyone else, and I've been through things you can't even imagine. My perspective might be different than yours, but that's exactly why it's so important to write it down and talk about it. If you're looking for a group of people who will just agree with you, then this isn't the place for that. This is a place for discussion, and differing opinions heard with respect as we tackle the many issues of today's world. My perspective is different because I'm seeing this through a completely different lens of experience, but it's still just as valid. And I'd invite you to go ask to any of the many people I've helped, the people who have cried while shaking my hand because they were so grateful, whether or not I'm a leader. They'll say yes, absolutely. I may not have spoken much up until now, but when I do speak, I expect those around me, especially those who consider themselves thought-leaders and problem solvers and humanitarians actively participating in a discussion – you – to listen. I may not speak often, but when I choose to speak, it's because what I have to say is important."

Silence

Then one of the other people banged their fist against the table, "yeah!"

People clapped.

I by no means wanted to shame that moderator or make a scene, but they were out of line acting like my opinion didn't matter. I had to stand up. I had to speak out not just for myself, but also for people like me.

No one gets to tell me – or you – that we can't do something.

I'm not willing to be ignored. I'm not willing to have my opinion or perspective belittled.

Don't ever let someone make you feel less worthy. You deserve to be in the room and you deserve to be heard. And if someone tries to make you feel less worthy, DO NOT give them credit by accepting it. Stand up. If it doesn't work, leave. Walk away.

We all have limited time and energy. Let's not spend what little we have on someone who tries to make us feel small.

That leadership group is something they do every year, with different people chosen for each cohort. The next year I was one of eight people asked to go back and give my two cents briefly to the next group at their own first meeting.

The question we were asked was: What was the best part of being in the group, or what advice do you have for them?

Well, the other seven people, some from my group, some from previous groups, spoke mostly about connection. They all spoke well and to some degree about how the best part was meeting other people from all over the state, all of us working on cool projects and the collaborations that could happen, and staying in touch afterwards. In a word: networking.

That's great, and true, and I felt that way too, but because there were other people talking about it I thought I'd do something a little different with my answer.

Shaking like a leaf, I stood up and said: "I don't want your experience to be like mine was."

The person who leads the groups each year, and had been the

137

one to ask me to come speak, look startled. I gave her an apologetic look and shrugged.

They were just starting their group, so I told them how during the first few sessions of our group, I barely spoke. I told them everything I just told you, about the Imposter Syndrome, feeling out of place, feeling unworthy, and then the epiphany and how much I enjoyed the last couple meetings because that Imposter Syndrome had lessened and I was more confident sharing my perspective.

I told them they had been chosen out of all the other people in the state, and they deserved to be there, in that room, with those other leaders. They deserved to be heard and it needed to be an open and respectful dialogue of everyone's different experiences and perspectives if it was going to work.

Then I sat back down in my chair, expecting nothing because surprisingly no one except me had clapped for any of the previous speakers.

Clap…clap, clap, clap

They were applauding.

I looked up and people were clapping and nodding their heads and one girl was crying.

Remember that chapter about how helpful it is to everyone if we're more open and honest and talk about our struggles? Remember how I said it'd help make us not feel so alone as we realize that others are going through the same or similar things?

Well, people came up to me at the end of the event and shook my hand, some of them with tears rolling down their cheeks. These people said it was EXACTLY what they'd been feeling during their first meeting as part of the group and they thought they were the only ones. Now they were all more connected just by the fact they could openly admit to themselves and one another that they were experiencing Imposter Syndrome and feeling out of place.

Don't ever doubt you are worthy and have a valid, albeit different, perspective. Don't let anyone make you feel small, including yourself. If someone else tries to make you feel small, don't let them. Don't give their negativity credit.

If you're at a networking event, or you've been selected for a special group, you've won an award, or you're attending some event, then feel confident in the fact that you're already in the room. That's the hardest part! You got there somehow and were chosen for a reason; so don't let your Imposter Syndrome hold you back from enjoying the experience and getting the most out of it.

You are by no means the only person there who is feeling that way. Be open about it (without dwelling on it) and push past those feelings of doubt.

The people who chose you have confidence in you. They chose you for a reason. They already know you're worthy.

The goal is to get yourself to feel that way too.

25
Final Thoughts

Self-doubt is an internal enemy. It's a battle raging inside you, and therefore you are the only one who can change it. You can be told all the techniques and science and advice and anecdotes in the world, but it's still YOU who has to put those into action, in your own way, for your own circumstances, to help you crush your self-doubt and gain more confidence.

- People who are happier are more confident.
- People who are calmer are more confident.
- People who are focused are more confident.
- People who are healthier are more confident.
- People who connect socially are more confident.

Want more confidence? Focus on these parts of your life mentioned above.

What do you need to do to be happier? Make it a priority and do the things that make your soul sing, plus the tips from this book. Write or say 10+ things every day for which you're grateful. Say positive "I am" statements every morning. Watch funny videos and do whatever you can to smile and laugh more often.

What do you need to do to be calmer? For me, I lower my cortisol levels by striking a power pose. I breathe from my belly and focus on my breaths for five minutes. I stretch. I write down my anxieties or talk it out with someone. I take calming supplements like magnesium, l-theanine, and drink lavender-chamomile tea. I go for a walk! I take a hot shower or bath.

What about your focus? Meditation is the key to this, but it's even better if you're doing it while trying to *balance*. Balancing on something, whether it's one foot or a ball or a beam, forces your brain to focus on that one thing. This then helps train your brain how to do that better when it comes to other activities. So if you're feeling like you can't focus, spend a few minutes trying to balance and breathing deeply.

Getting yourself healthier is a tricky one, especially coming from someone who is chronically ill. What it means, though, isn't that you need to be perfectly healthy to be happy and have more confidence, but you need to prioritize your health. If you have diabetes, you need to monitor and take care of it. If you have a chronic illness, you need to see doctors, get fourth and fifth opinions, and try treatments. If your weight is an issue then try to eat a little better and exercise a little more. You don't necessarily have to "diet," but start with just one or two days a week where you have a salad for lunch, or start by not allowing yourself dessert unless it's a weekend, etc. Small, consistent steps are going to be much better than large, inconsistent ones. Your health is literally your life, so make it a priority. Go for the walk if you can. Eat a little better. Sit a little less. Limit your screen time. Etc.

When it comes to connecting socially, it's surprisingly important for a number of areas of your life and well-being. As an introvert sometimes I secretly despise this, but you can't run from it. We need social interaction to function properly and it also happens to be one of the key components to happiness, health, and confidence. So get out there and do it a little more, or even just call a loved one to talk.

All these things are vastly important and often overlooked. So is your self-doubt.

I had no idea how much my internal voice was being a jerk to me until I finally started paying attention to it. Whoa. What a witch she was for a while. She didn't go down easily, either. She still rears her ugly side sometimes and I have to listen and pay attention

141

to realize she's back to whispering her negative words in my ears. Then, when I do realize it, I flip the script. I FORCE her to say nice things and rattle off my positive statements until it shuts her down.

It's almost like there's two voices in there, the positive one that I have control over, and the negative one that I have less control over. When the negative one starts whispering, it can feel so natural and go unnoticed and the negative way you feel about yourself is just a part of who you are. That's when you have to make the positive voice, the voice you control, SHOUT.

I AM CAPABLE.

I AM IMPORTANT.

I AM STRONG.

I AM WORTHY.

I AM LOVED.

You don't necessarily need to control that negative voice, what you're really doing is interrupting it and not giving it a chance to speak, until finally it just quits.

I wish I could tell you that once it's gone, it's gone for good, but you know better than that. That's why it's so important to make the techniques in this book, especially the quick and easy ones, part of your daily routine. When done regularly, these practices will train your brain to be happier, calmer, more focused, and more confident. They will help you overcome the struggles you're having now and then help *prevent* future issues.

It's only because of these techniques and training that I'm still alive today.

It's because of these techniques that I haven't had a full-blown panic attack in years, when I used to have them daily.

It's because of these practices that I can have a good relationship, a child, my own business, be a speaker, and write these books.

I'm not tooting my own horn here. What I'm saying is: If I can go from where I was to where I am now, you definitely can too.

I'm still a work in progress, but the person I want to be

and the person I am right now continue to get closer and closer together.

And that, my friends, is what we should all strive to accomplish. That is the key to a happier, more confident life. If we're not focused on that, nothing else matters.

I hope you agree, and I hope this book has been helpful. If it has, I hope you'll spread it around.

We could all use a little extra help, a boost. We could all be a little happier and more confident, and if we were, I think the world would be a better place.

Let's make it happen. Together.

26

About the Author: Corrina Thurston

Corrina Thurston is an artist, speaker, and author. She is known as the "Colored Pencil Artist" for the way she makes the medium of colored pencil come alive with vibrant colors and fine details in her stunning wildlife artwork.

Corrina began drawing in 2010, two years after falling chronically ill. Her drawings began as a therapeutic outlet until she registered as a business in 2015. After her first book, **How To Build Your Art Business with Limited Time or Energy**, she began speaking at galleries, nonprofits, and other organizations about art marketing, business, and entrepreneurship.

Corrina gave a TEDx Talk called "Why we should teach gratitude in school" in 2019 and has recently been speaking and teaching about happiness, confidence, and how to manage things like anxiety, depression, and self-doubt, which is how the idea for this book was developed.

Learn more about Corrina on her website: www.corrinathurston.com

27

Other books by Corrina Thurston

How To Build Your Art Business with Limited Time or Energy is Corrina's first book, focusing on exactly what the title says. It is another straightforward book, written in Corrina's signature conversational style, to help artists and creatives of all types build their creative businesses and grow their audiences. Learn more on her website: www.corrinathurston.com/books-2

How To Communicate Effectively – For Artists & Creatives is Corrina's second book, all about how to effectively **market** your creative work. From artist statements to blogging to grant-writing and reaching out to the media, Corrina covers many aspects of how to best market and promote your creative work and gain more customers/sales. Learn more on her website: www.corrinathurston.com/books-2

Find Your Happiness – Although not a book, you can check out the blog and other resources at FindYourHappiness.info Corrina has put together for anyone looking to try and live a happier life. From small adjustments to big changes, the site covers a lot of information and it's constantly being updated.